*I have made a great mistake. I have wasted my life
with mineralogy, which has led to nothing. Had I
devoted myself to birds, their life and plumage,
I might have produced something worth doing.*

JOHN RUSKIN

PL. CXIII

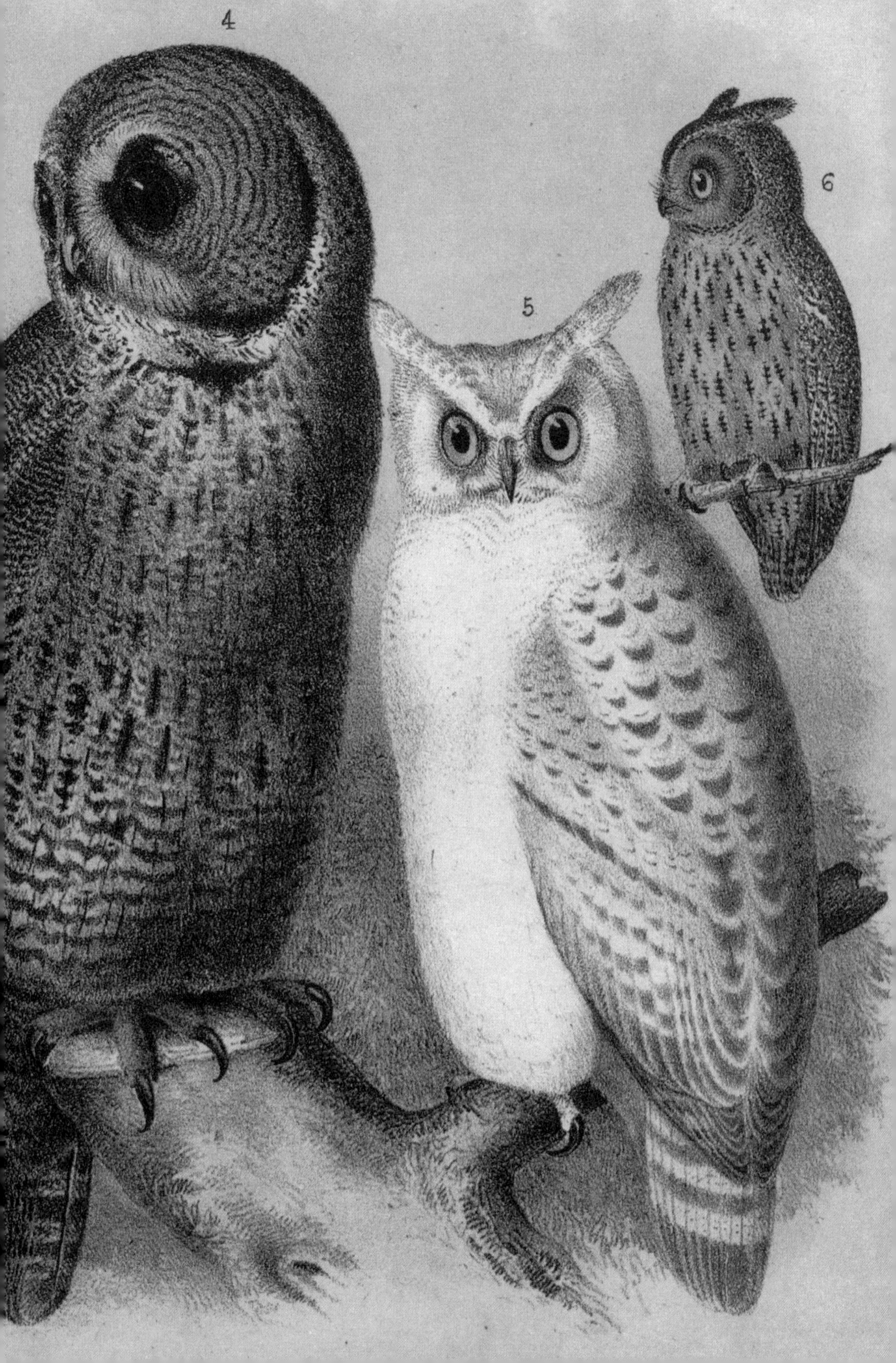

The

BEDSIDE BOOK

of BIRDS

~ An Avian Miscellany

GRAEME GIBSON

~ *Book design by CS Richardson*

Anchor Canada

FOR PEGGY, GRAEME, JESS AND MATTHEW

INTRODUCTIONS COPYRIGHT © 2005 MYSTERIOUS STARLING INC.
ANCHOR CANADA EDITION 2006

Pages 346–364 constitute a continuation of the copyright page.

Library and Archives Canada Cataloguing in Publication has been applied for.

ISBN-13: 978-0-385-66295-6
ISBN-10: 0-385-66295-5

Printed and bound in Canada
Printed on paper that does not contain any materials from trees of old-growth forests.

Published in Canada by
Anchor Canada, a division of
Random House of Canada Limited

Visit Random House of Canada Limited's website: www.randomhouse.ca

FRI 10 9 8 7 6 5 4 3 2 1

PAGE I: *Sunbittern*, E. Demonte (1931–2004), Brazil
PAGES II-III: *Owls*, T. Jasper (19th century), United States
TITLE PAGES: *Saddle-Back*, J.G. Keulemans (1842–1912), Netherlands/England

Night Crow

When I saw that clumsy crow
Flap from a wasted tree,
A shape in the mind rose up:
Over the gulfs of dream
Flew a tremendous bird
Further and further away
Into a moonless black
Deep in the brain, far back.

Theodore Roethke

The language of birds is very ancient, and,
like other ancient modes of speech, very
elliptical: little is said, but much is meant
and understood.

Gilbert White

Contents

Kakapo or Owl Parrot, J.G. Keulemans (1842–1912), Netherlands/England

INTRODUCTION

I CAME TO THE BIRDS relatively late in life. For almost thirty-seven years I didn't understand birdwatching. I remember how eccentric, how curious—even mysterious—I found the activity. Who were these tens of thousands of people with sensible shoes, a predilection for paramilitary raingear, and an almost risible devotion to birds?

Some collect species for their "life list" (that compilation of all the birds one has seen in a lifetime); they are chasers, for whom birding is a competitive sport. Some are scientists, and others work on nesting maps, migration monitoring or bird banding. For the majority of enthusiasts, however, birdwatching simply provides a personal and very special entrée into the natural world.

YEARS AGO I FOUND MYSELF sheltering by the wheelhouse on the *Cachalote*, a 52-foot motorsailer cruising in the Galapagos. A metallic sea was rising beneath sullen clouds that shredded themselves against the hills of Isabella Island. Everything was grey and black, and the ship was pitching uncomfortably.

Great Auk, artist unknown

I hadn't been expecting to see my first albatross until later, on Hood Island, where they nest. But in an abrupt clearing of the mist and driving rain, there it was, drifting low over the ragged sea. Enormous and powerful, effortless as sleep, it crossed our wake and then was gone in another squall. While some would say this sighting was merely luck, others might call it grace.

Suddenly any memory of whatever I might have learned about the albatross seemed irrelevant. It was enough to have seen it at that moment, and I was left with an enchanted sense that I had received a gift.

At its heightened moments, birdwatching can encourage a state of being close to rapture. It is an ecstasy that is said to accompany the writing of poetry; sometimes it comes when we're listening to music.

I suspect that, if I am fortunate enough to await death naturally, dreaming in a chair by some open window, the image of that Waved Albatross, with its great pale head and eight-foot wingspan, will still be a source of gratitude and wonder to me.

WHEN I FIRST WROTE ABOUT THE Waved Albatross, the idea of compiling a selection of writing that explored the ways in which humans have engaged themselves with birds began to grow in my mind. With the zeal of a convert, I started taking note of, then collecting, and finally obsessively searching out texts that illustrated something—almost anything—about our shared response to birds.

This book is the result. It isn't so much about birds themselves as it is about the richly varied and sometimes very intimate relationships that we have established with them during the hundreds of thousands of years that we and they have shared life on earth. It is also about the often grimmer ways in which birds have been forced to relate to us.

Humans developed as a species in a world full of birds. Despite seeing images of the great flocks of waders and marsh birds in African wetlands, or the millions of nesting Black Guillemots, Kittiwakes, Common Murres, Puffins, and various species of Gulls on northern sea-cliffs, it remains hard for us to conceive just how omnipresent birds must have been in the lives of our forebears.

Somewhere along the way we identified ourselves with them, and came to associate birds with the realm of spirits, as opposed to that of bodies and their carnal appetites.

Perhaps for this reason there's an abundance of intriguing material about birds, from all times and all cultures. Not only do they feature in creation myths, in sagas and parables, in liturgies and in fairy tales, but poets, writers, story-tellers and artists in all ages have found them a fertile source of imagery and symbol.

In the end I decided to divide the book into nine sections—nine different habitats, if you like, where certain species are naturally gathered together.

Material within the sections is more instinctively arranged. I'd like the reader, in exploring my "habitats," to encounter the unexpected, just as one might when exploring a richly varied but unfamiliar woodland: because the trail is unpredictable and you can't see beyond the surrounding foliage, you never know quite what to expect.

You might even discover some unanticipated aspect of self; for birds, in dream theory, are symbols for the personality of the dreamer.

GRAEME GIBSON

Published May 1 1802 by Cadell & Davies Strand.

Swallows certainly sleep all winter. A number of them conglobulate together, by flying round and round, and then all in a heap throw themselves under water, and lye in the bed of a river.

Samuel Johnson

I ~

"Oh, the Birds..."

Birds observed and recorded

Superb Lyrebird, S.J. Neele (1758–1824), England

I was coming to the end of a week scouting for a series of birding trips in Cuba's Zapata swamp, the vast area of marshland, reed-beds and low mixed forest that surrounds the Bay of Pigs. My companions were Orlando Garrido, Cuba's senior ornithologist, and Rogelio, an excellent forest warden and a wonderful man. At our last breakfast, with the Bay a limpid turquoise beyond a crescent beach and the air resounding with the gargling of Cuban crows, Garrido told me that Rogelio had a special surprise for us. They both grinned knowingly but neither would elaborate.

Later that morning, just off an old logging road, Garrido pointed to a tangle of sticks about twelve metres up in a nondescript tree. It was the nest of a Gundlach's Hawk, with the white and woolly shape of a nestling on its edge. Discovered just two days earlier, it was only the fourth official nesting site found in the twentieth century.

As we circled to the other side we saw the adult's rounded tail, then the whole bird. Watching us out of a cautious red eye, she'd frozen completely. Although her throat trembled, she didn't even blink.

The Gundlach's is a fine, strong bird, very much like our Cooper's Hawk. It is an endangered species endemic to Cuba, and only a handful of other people had ever seen one on the nest. All of us, I think, were sobered; certainly we were quiet.

On the way back it occurred to me that there were undoubtedly more skins of Gundlach's Hawk in museums around the world than there were live birds in the whole of Cuba. In the nineteenth century, most people treated birds as if they were stamps waiting to be included in a prize collection. As a result, countless thousands of birds and their eggs were collected. Considered a necessary part of scientific behaviour, this kind of killing was done by men as important as Audubon, who once wrote that he felt incomplete if he didn't kill a hundred birds a day.

As one of the first bird artists to use fresh models—which he meticulously posed after threading thin wires into their bodies—Audubon would sometimes kill a dozen individuals before finding the one he wanted. Most of us are defined by the age we live in—Audubon included—and in the nineteenth century birds were routinely slaughtered in astonishing numbers. Audubon reports that in a single day forty-eight thousand Golden Plovers were gunned down near New Orleans.

On May 28, 1854, William David Thoreau, who earned some of his keep by collecting specimens for science, wrote in his diary: "The inhumanity of science concerns me, as when I am tempted to kill a rare snake that I may ascertain its species. I feel that this is not the means of acquiring true knowledge."

But now, in the twenty-first century, I suspect that most bird-watchers would find it harder to identify a dead bird in the hand than a living one in flight.

When I think of the Gundlach's Hawk, it's the red eye I remember best, and that fluffy ball of a nestling. Despite being delighted and moved, I couldn't help feeling we shouldn't be there. We meant trouble for the mother and her young, and that brilliant red eye seemed to acknowledge it. We weren't the first to alarm her, and I feared we wouldn't be the last.

Sadly I was right: the following year I learned that her nestling had been captured, and after appropriate training in the disciplines of falconry, was being used to scare other birds away from the runways of Havana's international airport. I felt somehow culpable, and I still do when I remember.

One of the rewards of birdwatching is the brief escape it affords from our ancient and compelling need to make Nature useful. There may even be something of Thoreau's "true knowledge" in that evanescent taste of freedom.

G.G.

Clay vessel in the form of a bird, Mochica, Peru

greater yellowlegs

from The Wind Birds

THE RESTLESSNESS OF SHOREBIRDS, their kinship with the distance and swift seasons, the wistful signal of their voices down the long coastlines of the world make them, for me, the most affecting of wild creatures. I think of them as birds of wind, as "wind birds." To the traveler confounded by exotic birds, not to speak of exotic specimens of his own kind, the voice of the wind birds may be the lone familiar note in a strange land, and I have many times been glad to find them; meeting a whimbrel one fine summer day of February in Tierra del Fuego, I wondered if I had not seen this very bird a half-year earlier, at home. The spotted and white-rumped sandpipers, the black-bellied and golden plovers are birds of Sagaponack, but the spotted sandpiper has cheered me with its jaunty teeter on the Amazon and high up in the Andes (and so has its Eurasian counterpart, the common sandpiper, on the White Nile and in Galway and in the far-off mountains of New Guinea); one bright noon at the Strait of Magellan, the white-rump passed along the shore in flocks. I have seen golden plover on Alaskan tundra and in the cane fields of Hawaii, and heard the black-belly's wild call on wind-bright seacoast afternoons from Yucatán to the Great Barrier Reef.

Greater Yellowlegs, J.F. Lansdowne (1937–), Canada

The voice of the black-bellied plover carries far, a fluting melancholy *toor-a-lee* or *pee-ur-ee* like a sea bluebird, often heard before the bird is seen. In time of storm, it sometimes seems to be the only bird aloft, for with its wing span of two feet or more, the black-bellied plover is a strong flier; circumpolar and almost cosmopolitan, it migrates down across the world from breeding grounds within the Arctic Circle. Yet as a wanderer it is rivaled by several shorebirds, not least of all the sanderling of the Sagaponack beach, which ranks with the great skua and the Arctic tern as one of the most far-flung birds on earth.

The sanderling is the white sandpiper or "peep" of summer beaches, the tireless toy bird that runs before the surf. Because of the bold role it plays in its immense surroundings, it is the one sandpiper that most people have noticed. Yet how few notice it at all, and few of the fewer still who recognize it will ever ask themselves why it is there or where it might be going. We stand there heedless of an extraordinary accomplishment: the diminutive creature making way for us along the beaches of July may be returning from an annual spring voyage which took it from central Chile to nesting grounds in northeast Greenland, a distance of 8,000 miles. One has only to consider the life force packed tight into that puff of feathers to lay the mind wide open to the mysteries—the order of things, the why and the beginning. As we contemplate that sanderling, there by the shining sea, one question leads inevitably to another, and all questions come full circle to the questioner, paused momentarily in his own journey under the sun and sky.

PETER MATTHIESSEN (1927–), United States

LET US RETURN TO THE INSECTS

AMONG THE SINGERS in the July gloaming, one alone, were he able to vary his notes, could vie with the Toad's harmonious bells. This is the little Scops-owl, that comely nocturnal bird of prey, with the round golden eyes. He sports on his forehead two small feathered horns which have won for him in the district the name *Machoto banarudo*, the Horned owl. His song, which is rich enough to fill by itself the still night air, is of a nerve-shattering monotony. With imperturbable

Scops Owl, F.O. Morris (1810–1893), Ireland/England

9

and measured regularity, for hours on end, *kew, kew,* the bird spits out its cantata to the moon.

One of them has arrived at this moment, driven from the plane-trees in the square by the din of the rejoicings, to demand my hospitality. I can hear him in the top of a cypress near by. From up there, dominating the lyrical assembly, at regular intervals he cuts into the vague orchestration of the Grasshoppers and the Toads.

His soft note is contrasted intermittently, with a sort of Cat's mew, coming from another spot. This is the call of the Common Owl, the meditative bird of Minerva. After hiding all day in the seclusion of a hollow olive-tree, he started on his wanderings when shades of evening began to fall. Swinging along with a sinuous flight, he came from somewhere in the neighbourhood to the pines in my enclosure, whence he mingles his harsh mewing, slightly softened by distance, with the general concert.

The Green Grasshopper's clicking is too faint to be clearly perceived amidst these clamourers; all that reaches me is the least ripple, just noticeable when there is a moment's silence. He possesses as his apparatus of sound only a modest drum and scraper, whereas they, more highly privileged, have their bellows, the lungs, which send forth a column of vibrating air. There is no comparison possible. Let us return to the insects.

J. HENRI FABRE (1823–1914), France
from *The Life of the Grasshopper*

THE PARROT

ONLY INDIA PRODUCES THE PARROT, a bird green in colour, with a reddish collar and a large tongue broader than that of other birds, as a result of which it can articulate spoken words so clearly that if you did not see it you would think it was a person talking . . . Its beak is so hard that if it was thrown from a great height onto a stone, it would be saved when it rapped its beak and it would use it like a kind of buffer of extraordinary strength. Its whole head is so tough that if it needs to be admonished with blows when it is being taught to speak like people, it must be beaten with an iron rod. It learns more quickly and remembers better if it is taught and instructed when it is a chick up to within the second year of its life; but if it is at all older, it is forgetful and unteachable.

PETERBOROUGH BESTIARY

Parrot, Peterborough Bestiary MS53 (early 14th century)

Birds on the Western Front

CONSIDERING THE ENORMOUS economic dislocation which the war operations have caused in the regions where the campaign is raging, there seems to be very little corresponding disturbance in the bird life of the same districts. Rats and mice have mobilized and swarmed into the fighting line, and there has been a partial mobilization of owls, particularly barn owls, following in the wake of the mice, and making laudable efforts to thin out their numbers, What success attends their hunting one cannot estimate; there are always sufficient mice left over to populate one's dug-out and make a parade-ground and race-course of one's face at night. In the matter of nesting accommodation the barn owls are well provided for; most of the still intact barns in the war zone are requisitioned for billeting purposes, but there is a wealth of ruined houses, whole streets and clusters of them, such as can hardly have been available at any previous moment of the world's history since Nineveh and Babylon became humanly desolate. Without human occupation and cultivation there can have been no corn, no refuse, and consequently very few mice, and the owls of Nineveh cannot have enjoyed very good hunting; here in Northern France the owls have desolation and mice at their disposal in unlimited quantities, and as these birds breed in winter as well as in summer, there should be a goodly output of war owlets to cope with the swarming generations of war mice.

Apart from the owls one cannot notice that the campaign is making any marked difference in the bird life of the country-side. The vast flocks of crows and ravens that one expected to find in the neighbourhood of the fighting line are non-existent, which is perhaps rather a pity. The obvious explanation is that the roar and crash and fumes of high explosives have driven the crow tribe in panic from the fighting area; like many obvious explanations, it is not a correct one. The crows of the locality are not attracted to the battle-field, but they certainly are not scared away from it. The rook is normally so gun-shy and nervous where noise is concerned that the sharp banging of a barn door or the report of a toy pistol will sometimes set an entire rookery in commotion; out here I have seen him sedately busy among the refuse heaps of a battered village, with shells bursting at no great distance, and the impatient-sounding, snapping rattle of machine-guns going on all round him; for all the notice that he took he might have been in some peaceful English meadow on a sleepy Sunday afternoon. Whatever else German frightfulness may have done it has not frightened the rook of North-Eastern France; it has made his nerves steadier than they have ever been before, and future generations of small boys, employed in scaring rooks away from the sown crops in this region, will have to invent something in the way of super-frightfulness to achieve their purpose. Crows and magpies are nesting well within the shell-swept area, and over a small beech-copse I once saw a pair of crows engaged in hot combat with a pair of sparrow-hawks, while considerably higher in the sky, but almost directly above them, two Allied battle-planes were engaging an equal number of enemy aircraft.

Unlike the barn owls, the magpies have had their choice of building sites considerably restricted by the ravages of war; the whole avenues of poplars, where they were accustomed to construct their nests, have been blown to bits, leaving nothing but dreary-looking rows of shattered and splintered trunks to show where once they stood. Affection for a particular tree has in one case induced a pair of magpies to build their bulky, domed nest in the battered remnants of a poplar of which so little remained standing that the nest looked almost bigger than the tree; the effect rather suggested an archiepiscopal enthronement taking place in the ruined remains of Melrose Abbey. The magpie, wary and suspicious in his wild state, must be rather intrigued at the change that has come over the erstwhile fearsome not-to-be-avoided human, stalking everywhere over the earth as its possessor, who now creeps about in screened and sheltered ways, as chary of showing himself in the open as the shyest of wild creatures.

The buzzard, that earnest seeker after mice, does not seem to be taking any war risks, at least I have never seen one out here, but kestrels hover about all day in the hottest parts of the line, not in the least disconcerted, apparently, when a promising mouse area suddenly rises in the air in a cascade of black or yellow earth. Sparrow-hawks are fairly numerous, and a mile or two back from the firing line I saw a pair of hawks that I took to be red-legged falcons, circling over the top of an oak-copse. According to investigations made by Russian naturalists, the effect of the war on bird life on the

Eastern front has been more marked than it has been over here. "During the first year of the war rooks disappeared, larks no longer sang in the fields, the wild pigeon disappeared also." The skylark in this region has stuck tenaciously to the meadows and crop-lands that have been seamed and bisected with trenches and honeycombed with shell-holes. In the chill, misty hour of gloom that precedes a rainy dawn, when nothing seemed alive except a few wary waterlogged sentries and many scuttling rats, the lark would suddenly dash skyward and pour forth a song of ecstatic jubilation that sounded horribly forced and insincere. It seemed scarcely possible that the bird could carry its insouciance to the length of attempting to rear a brood in that desolate wreckage of shattered clods and gaping shell-holes, but once, having occasion to throw myself down with some abruptness on my face, I found myself nearly on the top of a brood of young larks. Two of them had already been hit by something, and were in rather a battered condition, but the survivors seemed as tranquil and comfortable as the average nestling.

At the corner of a stricken wood (which has had a name made for it in history, but shall be nameless here), at a moment when lyddite and shrapnel and machine-gun fire swept and raked and bespattered that devoted spot as though the artillery of an entire Division had suddenly concentrated on it, a wee hen-chaffinch flitted wistfully to and fro, amid splintered and falling branches that had never a green bough left on them. The wounded lying there, if any of them noticed the small bird, may well have wondered why anything having wings and no pressing reason for remaining should have chosen to stay in such a place. There was a battered orchard alongside the stricken wood, and the probable explanation of the bird's presence was that it had a nest of young ones whom it was too scared to feed, too loyal to desert. Later on, a small flock of chaffinches blundered into the wood, which they were doubtless in the habit of using as a highway to their feeding grounds; unlike the solitary hen-bird, they made no secret of their desire to get away as fast as their dazed wits would let them. The only other bird I ever saw there was a magpie, flying low over the wreckage of fallen tree-limbs; "one for sorrow," says the old superstition. There was sorrow enough in that wood.

The English gamekeeper, whose knowledge of wild life usually runs on limited and perverted lines, has evolved a sort of religion as to the nervous debility of even the hardiest game birds; according to his beliefs a terrier trotting across a field in which a partridge is nesting, or a mouse-hawking kestrel hovering over the hedge, is sufficient cause to drive the distracted bird off its eggs and send it whirring into the next county.

The partridge of the war zone shows no signs of such sensitive nerves. The rattle and rumble of transport, the constant coming and going of bodies of troops, the incessant rattle of musketry and deafening explosions of artillery, the night-long flare and flicker of star-shells, have not sufficed to scare the local birds away from their chosen feeding grounds, and to all appearances they have not been deterred from raising their broods. Gamekeepers who are serving with the colours might seize the opportunity to indulge in a little useful nature study.

SAKI (1870–1916), Burma/England

CARDINAL

Outside my window is a cardinal. There is no way of writing this sentence without dragging in its tow whole libraries of literary allusions. The frame of the window and the margins of the page entrap the bird that serves as a sign for any bird, just as any bird serves as a sign for any idea. Noah's dove, Macbeth's rooks, Horace's swans, Omar Khayyam's pigeons, Theocritus's nightingale, Count Fosco's canaries—they are no longer birds but usages of birds, feathered with words and meaning. My cardinal of symbolic colour and symbolic name bleeds now across this page as it did a moment ago across the sky. I wonder, corrupt with reading, if there ever was a moment when this sentence—*outside my window is a cardinal*—was not an artifice; when the blood-red bird on a steel-blue tree was quietly surprising, and nothing urged me to translate it, to domesticate it into a textual enclosure, to become its literary taxidermist. I wonder if there ever was a moment when a cardinal outside my window sat there in blazing splendour signifying nothing.

ALBERTO MANGUEL (1948–), Argentina/Canada

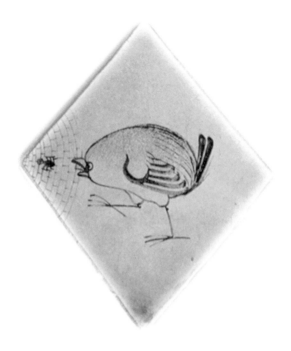

B Flat

Sing softly, Muse, The Reverend Henry White
Who floats through time as lightly as a feather
Yet left one solitary gleam of light
Because he was the Selbourne naturalist's brother

And told him once how on warm summer eaves
When moonlight filled all Fyfield to the brim
And yearning owls were hooting to their loves
On church and barn and oak-trees leafy limb

Wren and spider detail from stained glass window at Zouche Chapel, York Minster
(15th century), England

He took a common half-a-crown pitch pipe
Such as the masters used for harpsichords
And through the village trod with silent step
Measuring the notes of those melodious birds

And found that each one sang, or rather hooted,
Precisely in the measure of B flat.
And that is all that history has noted;
We know no more of Henry White but that.

So, softly, Muse in harmony and conformity
Pipe up for him and all such gentle souls
Thus in the world's enormousness, enormity,
So interested in music and in owls;

For though we cannot claim his crumb of knowledge
Was worth much more than virtually nil
Nor hail him for vast enterprise or courage,
Yet in my mind I see him walking still

With eager ear beneath his clerical hat
Through Fyfield village sleeping dark and blind,
Oh surely as he piped his soft B flat
The most harmless, the most innocent of mankind.

DOUGLAS STEWART (1913–1985),
New Zealand / Australia

The Raven, Le Corbeau Buff

THIS BIRD HAS ALWAYS BEEN FAMOUS; but its bad reputation has been owing, most probably, to its being confounded with other birds, and loaded with their ill qualities. It has ever been regarded most disgusting. Filth and rotten carcasses, it is said, are its chief food; and when it gluts its appetite on live prey, its victims are the weak or useful animals, lambs, leverets, etc., yet it sometimes attacks the large animals with success, supplying its want of strength and agility by cunning; it plucks out the eyes of buffaloes, and then, fixing on the back, it tears off the flesh deliberately: and what renders the ferocity more detestable, it is not incited by the cravings of hunger, but by the appetite for carnage . . .

GEORGES LOUIS LECLERC,
COMTE DE BUFFON (1707–1788), France

THE RAVEN.

The Raven, G.L. Leclerc, Comte de Buffon (1707–1788), France

from The Naturalist on the River Amazons

The Curl-crested Toucan (Pteroglossus Beauharnaisii).
—Of the four smaller Toucans, or Arassaris, found near Ega,
the Pteroglossus flavirostris is perhaps the most beautiful in
colours, its breast being adorned with broad belts of rich
crimson and black; but the most curious species, by far, is the
Curl-crested, or Beauharnais Toucan. The feathers on the
head of this singular bird are transformed into thin, horny
plates, of a lustrous black colour, curled up at the ends, and
resembling shavings of steel or ebony-wood: the curly crest
being arranged on the crown in the form of a wig. Mr.
Wallace and I first met with this species, on ascending the
Amazons, at the mouth of the Solimoens; from that point it
continues as a rather common bird on the terra firma, at least

Wooden toucan folk art, artist unknown (contemporary)

on the south side of the river as far as Fonte Boa, but I did not hear of its being found further to the west. It appears in large flocks in the forests near Ega in May and June, when it has completed its moult. I did not find these bands congregated at fruit-trees, but always wandering through the forest, hopping from branch to branch among the lower trees, and partly concealed among the foliage. None of the Arassaris, to my knowledge, make a yelping noise like that uttered by the larger Toucans (Ramphastos); the notes of the curl-crested species are very singular, resembling the croaking of frogs. I had an amusing adventure one day with these birds. I had shot one from a rather high tree in a dark glen in the forest, and entered the thicket where the bird had fallen to secure my booty. It was only wounded, and on my attempting to seize it, set up a loud scream. In an instant, as if by magic, the shady nook seemed alive with these birds, although there was certainly none visible when I entered the jungle. They descended towards me, hopping from bough to bough, some of them swinging on the loops and cables of woody lianas, and all croaking and fluttering their wings like so many furies. If I had had a long stick in my hand I could have knocked several of them over. After killing the wounded one, I began to prepare for obtaining more specimens and punishing the viragos for their boldness; but the screaming of their companion having ceased, they remounted the trees, and before I could reload, every one of them had disappeared.

Henry Walter Bates (1825–1892), England

Red Bird of Paradise,
T.W. Wood (1823–1903),
United States

HATCHETS, BEADS, KNIVES, AND HANDKERCHIEFS

MY FIRST BUSINESS was to send for the men who were accustomed to catch the Birds of Paradise. Several came, and I showed them my hatchets, beads, knives, and handkerchiefs; and explained to them as well as I could by signs, the price I would give for fresh-killed specimens. It is the universal custom to pay for everything in advance; but only one man ventured on this occasion to take goods to the value of two birds. The rest were suspicious, and wanted to see the result of the first bargain with the strange white man, the only one who had ever come to their island. After three days, my man brought me the first bird—a very fine specimen, and alive, but tied up in a small bag, and consequently its tail and wing feathers very much crushed and injured. I tried to explain to him, and to the others that came with him, that I wanted them as perfect as possible, and that they should either kill them, or keep them on a perch with a string to their leg. As they were now apparently satisfied that all was fair, and that I had no ulterior designs upon them, six others took away goods; some for one bird, some for more, and one for as many as six. They said they had to go a long way for them, and that they would come back as soon as they caught any. At intervals of a few days or a week, some of them would return, bringing me one or more birds; but though they did not bring any more in bags, there was not much improvement in their condition. As they caught them a long way off in the forest, they would scarcely ever come with one, but would tie it by the leg to a stick, and put it in their house till they caught another. The poor creature would make violent efforts to escape, would get among the ashes, or hang suspended by the leg till the limb was swollen and half-putrefied, and some-times die of starvation and worry. One had its beautiful head all defiled by pitch from a dammar torch; another had been so long dead that its stomach was turning green. Luckily, how-ever, the skin and plumage of these birds is so firm and strong, that they bear washing and cleaning better than almost any other sort; and I was generally able to clean them so well that they did not perceptibly differ from those I had shot myself.

Some few were brought me the same day they were caught, and I had an opportunity of examining them in all their beauty and vivacity. As soon as I found they were generally brought alive, I set one of my men to make a large bamboo cage with troughs for food and water, hoping to be able to keep some of them. I got the natives to bring me branches of a fruit they were very fond of, and I was pleased to find they ate it greedily, and would also take any number of live grasshoppers I gave them, stripping off the legs and wings, and then swallowing them. They drank plenty of water, and were in constant motion, jumping about the cage from perch to perch, clinging on the top and sides, and rarely resting a moment the first day till nightfall. The second day they were always less active, although they would eat as freely as before; and on the morning of the third day they were almost always found dead at the bottom of the cage, without any apparent cause. Some of them ate boiled rice as well as fruit and insects; but after trying many in succession, not one out of ten lived more than three days. The second or third day they would be dull and in several cases they were seized with convulsions and fell off the perch, dying a few hours afterwards. I tried immature as well as full-plumaged birds, but with no better success, and at length gave it up as a hopeless task, and confined my attention to preserving specimens in as good a condition as possible.

The Red Birds of Paradise are not shot with blunt arrows, as in the Aru Islands and some parts of New Guinea, but are snared in a very ingenious manner. A large climbing Arum bears a red reticulated fruit, of which the birds are very fond. The hunters fasten this fruit on a stout forked stick, and provide themselves with a fine but strong cord. They then seek out some tree in the forest on which these birds are accustomed to perch, and climbing up it fasten the stick to a branch and arrange the cord in a noose so ingeniously, that when the bird comes to eat the fruit its legs are caught, and by pulling the end of the cord, which hangs down to the ground, it comes free from the branch and brings down the bird. Sometimes, when food is abundant elsewhere, the hunter sits from morning till night under his tree with the cord in his hand, and even for two or three whole days in succession, without even getting a bite; while on the other hand, if very lucky, he may get two or three birds in a day. There are only eight or ten men at Bessir who practise this art, which is unknown anywhere else in the island. I determined, therefore, to stay as long as possible, as my only chance of getting a good series of specimens; and although I was nearly starved, everything eatable by civilized man being scarce or altogether absent, I finally succeeded.

ALFRED RUSSEL WALLACE (1823–1913), England
from *The Malay Archipelago*

OVERLEAF: Winged bird-headed divinities pollinating the sacred tree.
Stone relief. Mesopotamian, Nimrud. Neo-Assyrian.

THE BRUTE CHANGED HIS MIND

IN THE EVENING AFTER DINNER Mr Donkin and I were talking about birds and the speed of their flight. I always make a habit of pacing with my speedometer any bird which happened to fly alongside my motorcycle. My host, however, had the advantage of me here, for he owned an aeroplane, and when he got on to the subject of the flight of eagles he told me an amusing yarn. He told it with such enthusiasm and such vividness of recollection that I was, and still am, convinced of its accuracy. At the time of the incident there was staying as a guest at Meteor a certain Ronnie Adair, a flier who had achieved fame by making a safe landing after the engine and propeller of his plane had fallen off in mid-air. Here is the yarn as it was told to me.

"One day one of my boundary riders came in and reported that eagles were playing up with the lambing ewes in one of my paddocks. Ronnie immediately suggested that we have an aeroplane eagle-hunt. I had an old S.E. at the time, which I had bought just after the War; it had a maximum speed of 75 miles an hour. Ronnie took the controls; I climbed into the front cockpit with a twelve-gauge gun, and we flew over to where my man had reported that the eagles were bothering. When we arrived at the place we saw a big fellow get up at the far side of the paddock. We flew after it, and it turned to meet us. It seemed to want to know what on earth we were. Then it flew alongside, and seemed as interested in us as we were in it, for it kept turning its head and looking at the plane. The bus was flat out, doing its seventy-five; the eagle kept

Wedge-Tailed Eagle, H.C. Richter (1821–1902), England

level, and *never moved its wings*. Ronnie and I stared at it hard, and he will bear me out—it never moved a feather! This went on for two or three minutes. I shouted to Ronnie, 'How the hell is he doing it?' And he shouted back, 'I'm damned if I know! Why not dong him anyhow?' So I cocked the gun, and was just about to have a dong at him when the brute changed its mind and shot ahead. He just shot straight ahead and left us standing, and still he never batted his wings. Ronnie shouted that the damn thing was just laughing at us, and he was going home; so we turned round and came back to the house."

FRANCIS RATCLIFFE (1904–1970), India/Australia
from *Flying Fox and Drifting Sand*

from The Song of the Dodo

Stephens Island is a dot of land between the North Island and the South Island of New Zealand, and the extinction of this endemic wren, *Xenicus lyalli*, is just one more instance among many, tiny in its own scope but emblematic. The bird was a small thing with short wings and almost no tail, either totally flightless or nearly so. It made its living by skulking among rocks and feeding on insects. Even during good times, the species was perilously rare. Besides those disadvantages, presumably it suffered from ecological naïveté—being too trusting for its own good. We can't be confident whether or not it was totally flightless, nor just how disastrously trusting, because almost no one ever saw it alive.

Stephens Island Wren, D.M. Reid-Henry (1919–1977), Ceylon / England

It was discovered in 1894 by a lighthouse keeper named Lyall—or, to be more precise, it was discovered by one of Lyall's cats. The cat killed a local bird and proudly presented the carcass to its master, as cats will do. Lyall, being something of a birdwatcher, recognized that the stubby-winged creature was unusual and passed it along to an expert on New Zealand's birds. The expert in turn shipped the preserved specimen off to a British bird journal, along with a manuscript describing this new species and naming it, for the lighthouse keeper, *Xenicus lyalli*. With the wren now internationally famous, collectors arrived on Stephens Island. Apparently a combination of factors—collection, habitat destruction as the island's forest was cleared for pasture, and further predation by Lyall's cats—destroyed the entire population within a very short time.

Twelve specimens of *X. lyalli* now exist in museums. Back on Stephens Island itself, the bird has never been seen again.

DAVID QUAMMEN (1948–), United States

FROM JUNGLE PEACE

IN THE COURSE OF FIVE DAYS at New Amsterdam we achieved our object. We found hoatzins, their nests, eggs, and young, and perpetuated in photographs their wonderful habits handed down through all the ages past, from the time when reptiles were the dominant beings, and birds and mammals crept about, understudying their role to come, as yet uncertain of themselves and their heritage. When we needed it the sun broke through the rain and shone brightly; when our lenses were ready, the baby hoatzins ran the gamut of their achievements. They crept on all fours, they climbed with fingers and toes, they dived headlong, and swam as skillfully as any Hesperornis of old. This was, and I think always will be, to me, the most wonderful sight in the world. To see a tiny living bird duplicate within a few minutes the processes which, evolved slowly through uncounted years, have at last culminated in the world of birds as we find it today—this is impressive beyond words. No poem, no picture, no terrible danger, no sight of men killed or injured has ever affected me as profoundly as this.

WILLIAM BEEBE (1877–1962), United States

Hoatzin, E. Demonte (1931–2004), Brazil

34

Your image, tormenting and elusive,
I could not touch in the mist.
"God!" I said by mistake,
never thinking to say that myself.

God's name like a gigantic bird
flew out from my breast.
Before me thick mist swarms,
behind me stands an empty cage.

OSIP MANDELSTAM

II ~

IN THE BEGINNING

How long have we been enchanted by birds?
Forever it seems.

Aztec eagle warrior (detail), ceramic, Mexico

When an anonymous artist incised an owl in the cave at Chauvet, there were probably fewer people on earth than there are in the Greater Toronto area today. Every human being lived in a rich and productive ecosystem. Life was relatively easy, and would remain so for another twenty thousand years—until population growth and the evolution of farming introduced the unfortunate notion of hard work.

I've twice had the good fortune to visit an Arnhemland safari camp at Mount Borradaile, a ninety-minute flight east along the coast from Darwin in northern Australia. There the rock outcrops rising from a monsoon plain are intricately honeycombed with caves and grottos that contain an extraordinary collection of Aboriginal rock paintings. Some images date back more than fifty thousand years.

The caves are surprisingly fresh and dry in the tropical heat and heavy seasonal rains, which helps explain why people lived there for so long. There's also the "bush tucker," or wild food, which is varied and plentiful: Rock Ferns, Passion Fruit, and Native Gooseberries are tasty and nutritious; fish such as Barramundi still

Owl created in Chauvet Cave 30,000 years ago, France

teem in pools below the rapids; and as the dry season approaches, wading birds cluster together by shrinking waterholes. A knowledgeable person wouldn't have much trouble finding food or shelter in such a place. As a result, especially for someone accustomed to our relatively unforgiving northern forests, there's a sense of Eden—a Garden of Eden—and perhaps it really was like that—at least until the Europeans arrived.

Current research indicates that men in successful hunting-gathering societies spend about a week each month in search of game, and that women's work takes between one and three hours a day. The rest is leisure time, as we now call it. There's good reason to believe that ritual and ceremony, and probably language, occupied much of that time. The remarkable paintings at Chauvet, Lascaux, or Mount Borradaile, support this notion. Whatever else prompted such art, it seems probable that a ritualistic attempt to influence the hunt was involved.

An artistic people with time on their hands must have wondered about the meaning of things. Death, for instance: what was it that had departed the body and left it merely a corpse? And dreams—where did they come from? Was someone or something trying to instruct or warn us? And what, if anything, was out there, beyond the ring of firelight in which the people sat beneath a vast, clear sky at night?

Birds had been around for more than 150 million years by the time humans appeared on the scene. We came to self-awareness surrounded by them, and as there were few of us, birds would not yet have learned to fear us: as Charles Darwin and others discovered, they could have been knocked off their nests with a stick. Doubtless birds and their eggs were our first fast food.

And birds would have been present in great numbers. As recently as 1813, John James Audubon rode all day under a sky filled with migrating pigeons. He reckoned that a billion birds had flown past him by nightfall. In 1866, another legendary flight arrived in southern Ontario: over a mile wide, with an estimated two birds per square yard, it took fourteen hours to pass overhead. Subsequent estimates suggest there were more than three billion birds in that assembly.

Perhaps because they were common enough to be commonplace and were relatively easy to kill, birds are rare in paleolithic cave art, but they are vibrant players later, in myths and stories from all cultures. Finland's great national epic, the Kalevala, features a "beauteous duck" and her eggs, which become the earth and sky. In the north, loons and various other diving birds are credited with bringing mud up from the primordial sea so that dry land could be fashioned. Among the Yoruba, a hen with five claws spreads handfuls of earth until the seas are parted. Inanna, the Sumerian goddess of love, was depicted with wings; Horus of Egypt had the head of a falcon.

When St. Matthew's gospel described "the Spirit of God descending like a dove" and alighting on Jesus at his baptism, it was partaking of a tradition that reaches back into prehistoric times. So for that matter were the Mayans when they venerated Quetzalcoatl, their all-powerful plumed serpent. It is noteworthy that by the time of the Greeks the gods had been assigned two attributes possessed by birds, but not originally by men: flight and song. The more godlike you were, the more birdlike you were as well.

Man is the only singing primate; a fact that may cast some light on the ancient connection.

G.G.

Guillemot egg, artist unknown (possibly 19th century)

RAVEN

THE RAVEN IS THE FIRST BIRD to be mentioned by a specific name in the Bible, and its early appearance in the story of Noah's Ark (Genesis 8:7) makes it one of the first birds on written records. The raven holds claim to unwritten birdlore, too, for it is known all around the northern half of the globe, and has many a role in Nordic sagas, the legends of North American Indian tribes, and the folk tales told around desert campfires and Eskimo snow lodges.

Here in Genesis it is offered the role of messenger when Noah seeks to learn whether the glimpse of distant mountaintops means that there is enough dry land for his family to begin rebuilding homes, find food and growing things again. Only a bird would be able to bring back such word, yea or nay, and Noah must have thought that the raven—strong of wing and adventurous of spirit—would be the best choice. Then, too, its black wings would be easily followed by watchers at the Ark windows, even against gray skies, while those of a smaller or paler bird would be lost.

So Noah brought it to the window, his fingers cupped over the folded wings, then opened his hands to let the bird launch skyward with alternate flap and soaring glide—the typical raven flight pattern—and then disappear from sight. Presently those at the window could see it again, and it would continue to appear and disappear all through the day, but it did not return to the Ark, at least not while watchers at the Ark windows could see any shadow of wings against twilight sky. Then Noah must have remembered that raven is an eater of carrion and would have found plenty of such fare exposed by the falling waters . . . that it is a bird of the hill, not used to nesting in cotes along a garden wall, which the Ark resembled, and would not have had any need or instinct for returning to such quarters, as doves would do. The fault had been Noah's for making the wrong choice, but down through the ages the raven has had to bear the blame, becoming the symbol of ill omen and even death, the companion of witches and wizards and the embodiment of lost souls.

The raven's black feathers and ominous croak added to this superstitious aura, especially for ravens that learned to talk, and it permeated the beliefs of other religions besides the Judeo-Christian lore. But whatever evil clung to the raven's feathers from pagan tales was enhanced by its failure as messenger for Noah, and when other Bible lines seemed to say that God himself had to feed the raven fledglings, since their parents did not do so, the failure to return to the Ark was taken as proof that a raven has no care for mate or young.

Anyone who watched ravens would soon learn that these birds are loyal and considerate mates and devoted parents. You also learn that young raven nestlings squawk for food with louder and longer cries than almost any other species you could name, so they were the example that came immediately to mind when the writers of Job 38:41 and Psalm 147:7–9 wanted to call up a reminder of how God the Father

Raven.

Old Male.

Thick Shell bark Hickory.

Drawn from Nature by J.J. Audubon. F.R.S.F.L.S.

Lith.ᵈ Printed & Col.ᵈ by J.T. Bowen. Philad.

provides for all small wildlings, giving each its food—not with his own hand but by providing parent ravens—as he does almost all wild parents, beast or bird—with the instincts to choose the food best suited to infant needs, to bring such food again and again as long as the opened beaks and lifted voices reveal hunger's need. The newer translations that ask who provides the raven with its prey or quarry (rather than with its food, as in the King James Bible) give a clearer idea of God's role. Because young ravens cry with such persistent demand, parent ravens bring more and more food, often too much even for growing youngsters that consume their own weight in food each day—as most nestlings of all kinds do in order to reach full growth in such a brief span. Consequently, unneeded food is sometimes left untouched on the nest rim, or even pushed off to the ground below where some other hungry meat-eater may seize it for a welcome meal.

    . . . firm belief that the ravens brought both bread and meat to Elijah at God's command has remained a part of Judeo-Christian teaching, restoring some of the good name that this bird of blackness lost as Noah's unreturning messenger. And the lines from Job and the Psalms, declaring that God himself made feeding the ravens his special charge, were remembered all the more by Christians who read the Gospel according to St. Luke, finding in 12:24 this forthright command to observe these black-feathered birds and learn their ways, which were also the ways of the Lord:

Raven, J.J. Audubon (1785–1851), France / United States

*Consider the ravens: for they neither sow nor reap; which
have neither storehouse nor barn; and God feedeth them:
how much more are ye better than the fowls?*

In Matthew 6:26 the same scene is described, but with Jesus
asking his followers to look at all birds and so learn of a
Heavenly Father's care, not just at ravens. It seems possible
that Jesus spoke with both wordings. We can almost see him
there on the mountainside, the gray craggy rocks behind him
rising up like a throne against the blue sky, his voice low, but
clear and vibrant with the earnestness of his message.

"Behold the birds," he might have begun. "Look at the
birds." And then—perhaps—a familiar black shadow came
soaring into view, catching his eye for more specific example
so that he said, "Consider the raven. . . ."

VIRGINIA C. HOLMGREN (1909–2003), United States
from *Birdwalk Through the Bible*

CRANES

CRANES DIVIDE THE NIGHT into sentry-duties and they make up the sequence of the watches by order of rank, holding little stones in their claws to ward off sleep. When there is danger they make a loud cry.

PETERBOROUGH BESTIARY

Cranes, Peterborough Bestiary MS53 (early 14th century)

Mooin and the Seven Hunters

Mooin, the Bear, the Micmacs call the four stars of the Big Dipper, or the Great Bear, Ursa Major. The three stars of the handle of the dipper, or the tail of the Bear, they say are the first three of seven hunters who pursue the Bear across the northern sky during the warm summer months: Robin (because it is a reddish star), Chickadee (because it is small like a chickadee), and Moose Bird (Gray Jay). In the constellation Bootes are the four other hunters: Pigeon, Blue Jay (because it is a blue star), Owl (Koo-koo-gwesoo), and Saw-whet—the four that lose the chase as they drop from sight below the northern horizon in the late summer. Above the hunters is Mooin's den the group of stars of Corona Borealis. The tiny star beside Chickadee is his cooking pot which he carries along to cook the meat when Mooin is killed.

For generations on summer evenings the Micmacs watched the four stars of the Bear fleeing across the northern horizon trailed by the seven stars, whom they called the seven hunters. In the cold moons of winter they saw the same four stars of the Bear lying high in the sky. Then, as the earth turned warm in the spring, they watched the four stars descend the steep slopes of the heavens and again flee across the northern sky. The tale of Mooin and the seven hunters is a very old myth of the Micmacs and one which they told and still tell in the present tense because it is always happening.

In the spring Mooin in the sky awakes from her long winter sleep, leaves her den and comes down the steep hills to look for food. Chickadee sees her, but being little he cannot follow the trail alone and he calls for the other hunters. Together they start off with Chickadee and his cooking pot between Robin and Moose Bird. He is so little he might get lost in the great sky if Robin and Moose Bird were not there to look after him.

All summer Mooin runs across the northern sky and the hunters follow. But as autumn creeps into the summer nights the four hunters, Blue Jay, Saw-whet, Owl, and Pigeon, far behind the others, grow weary, and one by one they lose the trail. First Owl, Koo-koo-gwesoo, and Saw-whet drop by the way. But you must not laugh when you hear that Saw-whet fails to share in the meat, and you must not mock his rasping cry, for if you do, wherever you are, he will come in the night with his flaming torch of bark and burn the clothes that cover you. Then, Blue Jay and Pigeon lose the way, and in the crisp nights of autumn only Moose Bird and Chickadee and Robin, the hunters that are always hunting, are on the trail. At last Mooin grows weary of the long chase and is overtaken by Robin.

Brought to bay, Mooin rears to defend herself; Robin pierces her with his arrow, and she falls dead upon her back. Hungry from the long chase, and always thin in the autumn, Robin is eager for Mooin's fat. He leaps on her bleeding body and is covered with blood. Flying to the nearest maple in skyland he shakes off the blood—all except from his breast. "That," Chickadee tells him, "you will have as long as your name is Robin."

The blood that Robin shakes from his back spatters far

and wide over the trees on the earth below. Thus, every year, comes the red on the leaves, reddest on the maples because the maple in the sky receives the most blood. The sky, as you know, is just the same as the earth, only up above and older.

After Robin kills Mooin, Chickadee arrives, and together they cut the meat and cook it in Chickadee's pot. As they begin to eat Moose Bird arrives. He had almost lost the trail, but when he found it again he did not hurry. He knew it would take some time for the others to cut the meat and cook it, and he did not mind missing the work. Indeed he was so well pleased with lagging behind and arriving just as the food was ready that he has ever since ceased to hunt and follows the hunters sharing with them the spoils of the hunt. "He-who-comes-in-at-the-last-moment," Mikchagogwech he is called.

Robin and Chickadee being generous share their meat with Moose Bird, and together Robin and Moose Bird dance around the pot as Chickadee stirs the meat. And so did the old Micmacs in the old days when the Indians were brothers and shared their food.

All winter Mooin's skeleton lies on its back in the sky. But her life-spirit has entered another Mooin that lies on her back, invisible in the den, and sleeping the long sleep of winter. When spring touches the sky she will awake and come from her den, and will descend the steep slopes of the sky, and again will be chased by the hunters. In the chill days of autumn she will be slain, and will send her life-spirit into the body of a bear that lies invisible in the den. Thus life goes on from generation to generation. There is no end.

Traditional Micmac tale, Canada
in Robertson, *Red Earth*

Small Bird, K. Pootoogook (1935–), Nunavut / Canada

Gertrude's Bird

In those days when our Lord and St. Peter wandered upon earth, they came once to an old wife's house, who sat baking. Her name was Gertrude, and she had a red mutch on her head. They had walked a long way, and were both hungry, and our Lord begged hard for a bannock to stay their hunger. Yes, they should have it. So she took a tiny little piece of dough and rolled it out, but as she rolled it, it grew and grew till it covered the whole griddle.

Nay, that was too big; they couldn't have that. So she took a tinier bit still; but when that was rolled out it covered the whole griddle just the same, and that bannock was too big, she said; they couldn't have that either.

The third time she took a still tinier bit—so tiny you could scarce see it; but it was the same story over again—the bannock was too big.

"Well," said Gertrude, "I can't give you anything; you must just go without, for all these bannocks are too big."

Black Woodpecker, E. Demartini (dates and country unknown)

Then our Lord waxed wroth, and said,—

"Since you love me so little as to grudge me a morsel of food, you shall have this punishment,—you shall become a bird, and seek your food between bark and bole, and never get a drop to drink save when it rains."

He had scarce said the last word before she was turned into a great black woodpecker, or Gertrude's bird, and flew from her kneading-trough right up the chimney; and till this very day you may see her flying about, with her red mutch on her head, and her body all black, because of the soot in the chimney; and so she hacks and taps away at the trees for her food, and whistles when rain is coming, for she is ever athirst, and then she looks for a drop to cool her tongue.

Traditional Norwegian folktale
in Asbjørnsen and Moe, *East o' the Sun and West o' the Moon*

Common Potoo, P.H. Gosse (1810–1888), England

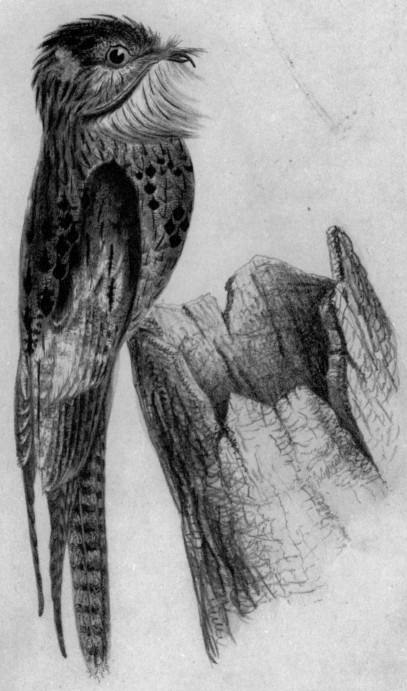

Plate VI.

P.H.G. del et lith.   Reeve, Benham & Reeve, imp.

Nyctibius Jamaicensis, *Gmel.*

(p. 44)

Extreme Tameness of the Birds

I WILL CONCLUDE MY DESCRIPTION of the natural history of these islands, by giving an account of the extreme tameness of the birds.

This disposition is common to all the terrestrial species; namely, to the mocking-thrushes, the finches, wrens, tyrant-flycatchers, the dove, and carrion-buzzard. All of them often approached sufficiently near to be killed with a switch, and sometimes, as I myself tried, with a cap or hat. A gun is here almost superfluous; for with the muzzle I pushed a hawk off the branch of a tree. One day, whilst lying down, a mocking-thrush alighted on the edge of a pitcher, made of the shell of a tortoise, which I held in my hand, and began very quietly to sip the water; it allowed me to lift it from the ground whilst seated on the vessel: I often tried, and very nearly succeeded, in catching these birds by their legs. Formerly the birds appear to have been even tamer than at present. Cowley (in the year 1684) says that the "Turtle-doves were so tame, that they would often alight upon our hats and arms, so as that we could take them alive: they not fearing man, until such time

Sombre Hummingbird, H.C. Richter (1821–1902), England

57

as some of our company did fire at them, whereby they were rendered more shy." Dampier also, in the same year, says that a man in a morning's walk might kill six or seven dozen of these doves. At present, although certainly very tame, they do not alight on people's arms, nor do they suffer themselves to be killed in such large numbers. It is surprising that they have not become wilder; for these islands during the last hundred and fifty years have been frequently visited by bucaniers and whalers; and the sailors, wandering through the woods in search of tortoises, always take cruel delight in knocking down the little birds.

These birds, although now still more persecuted, do not readily become wild: in Charles Island, which had then been colonized about six years, I saw a boy sitting by a well with a switch in his hand, with which he killed the doves and finches as they came to drink. He had already procured a little heap of them for his dinner; and he said that he had constantly been in the habit of waiting by this well for the same purpose. It would appear that the birds of this archipelago, not having as yet learnt that man is a more dangerous animal than the tortoise or the Amblyrhynchus, disregard him, in the same manner as in England shy birds, such as magpies, disregard the cows and horses grazing in our fields.

CHARLES DARWIN (1809–1882), England
from *The Voyage of the* Beagle

BROLGA, THE DANCING GIRL

BROLGA WAS THE FAVOURITE of everyone in the tribe, for she was not only the merriest among them, but also their best dancer. The other women were content to beat the ground while the men danced, but Brolga must dance; the dances of her own creation as well as those she had seen. Her fame spread and many came to see her. Some also desired her in marriage, but she always rejected them.

An evil magician, Nonega, was most persistent in his attention, until the old men of the tribe told him that, because of his tribal relationship and his unpleasant personality, they would never allow Brolga to become his wife. "If I can't have her," snarled Nonega, "she'll never belong to anyone else." For already he had planned to change her from a girl into some creature.

One day, when Brolga was dancing by herself on an open plain near her camp, Nonega, chanting incantations from the centre of a whirlpool in which he was travelling, enveloped the girl in a dense cloud of dust. There was no sign of Brolga after the whirlpool had passed, but standing in her place was

Brolga, P.A. Johnsgard (1931–), United States

a tall, graceful bird, moving its wings in the same manner as the young dancer had moved her arms. When they saw the resemblance everyone called out "Brolga! Brolga!" The bird seemed to understand and, moving towards them, bowed and performed even more intricate dances than before.

From that time onward the aborigines have called that bird Brolga, and they tell their children how the beautiful girl was transformed into the equally beautiful grey bird which still dances on the flood plains of northern Australia.

Traditional Australian myth
in Mountford, *The Dawn of Time*

from At Swim-Two-Birds

Extract from my typescript descriptive of Finn Mac Cool and his people, being humorous or quasi-humorous incursion into ancient mythology: Of the musics you have ever got, asked Conán, which have you found the sweetest?

I will relate, said Finn. When the seven companies of my warriors are gathered together on the one plain and the truant clean-cold loud-voiced wind goes through them, too sweet to me is that. Echo-blow of a goblet-base against the tables of the palace, sweet to me is that. I like gull-cries and the twittering together of fine cranes. I like the surf-roar at Tralee, the songs of the three sons of Meadhra and the whistle of Mac Lughaidh. These also please me, man-shouts at a parting, cuckoo-call in May. I incline to like pig-grunting in Magh Eithne, the bellowing of the stag of Ceara, the whinging of fauns in Derrynish. The low warble of water-owls in

Craft bird folk art, artist unknown (contemporary)

62

Loch Barra also, sweeter than life that. I am fond of wing-beating in dark belfries, cow-cries in pregnancy, trout-spurt in a lake-top. Also the whining of small otters in nettle-beds at evening, the croaking of small-jays behind a wall, these are heart-pleasing. I am friend to the pilibeen, the red-necked chough, the parsnip land-rail, the pilibeen móna, the bottle-tailed tit, the common marsh-coot, the speckle-toed guillemot, the pilibeen sléibhe, the Mohar gannet, the peregrine plough-gull, the long-eared bush-owl, the Wicklow small-fowl, the bevil-beaked chough, the hooded tit, the pilibeen uisce, the common corby, the fish-tailed mud-piper, the crúiskeen lawn, the carrion sea-cock, the green-lidded para-keet, the brown bog-martin, the maritime wren, the dove-tailed wheatcrake, the beaded daw, the Galway hill-bantam and the pilibeen cathrach. A satisfying ululation is the contending of a river with the sea. Good to hear is the chirping of little red-breasted men in bare winter and distant hounds giving tongue in the secrecy of fog. The lamenting of a wounded otter in a black hole, sweeter than harpstrings that. There is no torture so narrow as to be bound and beset in a dark cavern without food or music, without the bestowing of gold on bards. To be chained by night in a dark pit without company of chessmen—evil destiny! Soothing to my ear is the shout of a hidden blackbird, the squeal of a troubled mare, the complaining of wild-hogs caught in snow.

Relate further for us, said Conán.

It is true that I will not, said Finn.

FLANN O'BRIEN (1911–1966), Ireland

A Reputation for Lechery

THE SPARROW, "Venus' son," as Chaucer called the bird, has a reputation for lechery which still survives in the Victorian music-hall refrain "Me Old Cock-sparrow!" Like the dove, the sparrow was sacred to Venus, the goddess of love, and early natural historians declared that both birds had no equals for salacity. Modern ornithologists seem to agree with such findings, although some authorities maintain that "coition is normally solicited by the female."

Today we welcome the sparrow in our noisy polluted cities because it is one of the few birds prepared to nest cheerfully behind the bright hoardings of supermarkets or gas stations. Yet in 1559 a Lutheran pastor in Dresden implored the Elector of Saxony to help him exterminate the sparrows because of "their incessant and extremely vexatious chatterings, and scandalous acts of unchastity committed during the service, to the hindrance of God's Word and of Christian Doctrine." . . .

Sparrow, T.M. Shortt (1911–1986), Canada

The lascivious Devil might assume the form of a sparrow. When St. Dominic was preaching from behind a grille to some sisters in a Roman convent, warning them against the different shapes taken by devils to deceive the elect, a sparrow suddenly flew through the air and hopped on to the sisters' heads. According to Blessed Cecilia, the saint told one of the nuns to catch the bird and hand it to him. Holding the bird fast in one hand he

> commenced plucking off the feathers with the other, saying the while: "You wretch, you rogue!" When he had plucked him clean of all his feathers amid much laughter from the Brothers and Sisters, and awful shrieks of the sparrow, he pitched him out, saying: "Fly now if you can, enemy of mankind.". . . And so it came about that he employed for God's glory what the enemy of mankind had from envy done for their hurt and hindrance.

. . . Nymphomaniac witches transformed themselves into sparrows, and physicians declared that a roasted sparrow was a splendid aphrodisiac. "This is an undeniable Aphorism," said the seventeenth-century physician Culpepper, "that whatsoever any Creature is addicted unto, they move or incite the man or woman, that eats them, to the like; and therefore Partridges, Quails, Sparrows, etc. being extremely addicted to Venery, they work the same effect in those Men and Women that eat them."

BERYL ROWLAND (1918–2003), Scotland/Canada
from *Birds with Human Souls*

THE EGG

HERE IS WHAT THE FEMALE bird is able to accomplish in a mere twenty-four hours.

After one of the male's many sperm fertilizes the female's ripe ovum or egg, a small spot on the ovum—now a developing embryo—bursts through the ovary and slowly begins the journey down the meandering oviduct, a long and convoluted tube with elastic walls. During this journey, the egg as we know it—yolk, white, and enclosing shell—will be produced.

Peristaltic contractions of the muscle layers of the oviduct squeeze the developing egg into each of its five chambers in sequence. It is in the magnum of the oviduct that the egg receives its layer of albumen, a task taking about three hours. This albumen (the white part of the egg, as any chicken-egg eater can identify) surrounds the embryo and holds much of the water that is so important to the developing chick's survival.

When the magnum first secretes the albumen, it is a dense, jellylike layer. By the time the egg is laid, however, four separate layers of albumen are detectable. The first layer is thin and watery, a mixture within which the embryo may rotate. The next is a thicker one, surrounded by a fluid layer. The fourth is called the chalaza, a pair of dense, twisted "cords" of egg-white attached to opposite ends of the embryo

Guillemot eggs, artist unknown (possibly 19th century)

and yolk. It is the job of these cords to attach the embryo to the shell and enable it to turn as the incubating bird turns the egg.

The next step in the egg-producing process occurs in the isthmus where the egg receives its two shell membranes, the first surrounding the albumen, the outer membrane firmly attached to the shell itself.

Within the uterus itself, the shell is formed over the next nineteen to twenty hours. This porous structure is made up primarily of calcium carbonate. As a rule, the thickness of the shell is proportionate to its size, with larger eggshells being thicker than smaller ones. The egg colors, if any, are produced here.

Once the shell is added, through the laying process, and thereafter over the course of its incubation, the chick must receive all its nutrients from the contents of the egg, including calcium from the shell. In many birds, the yolk, the primary source of nutrition, is almost depleted by the time the young bird hatches.

Oxygen is absorbed through the shell into the egg and carbon dioxide is expelled through blood vessels in the embryo and membrane, and out through tiny pores in the shell, for the chick must be able to breathe if it is to metabolize food.

The egg even contains a sac for the chick's waste products, allowing waste to be kept separate from the unused food sources.

When the egg is fully formed, its mother has produced a nearly perfect environment for her developing chick.

LESTER SHORT (1933–), United States

TROGON RESPLENDENS.
Resplendent Trogon.

FROM POPUL VUH
(THE QUICHÉ MAYAN BOOK OF CREATION)

THIS IS THE BEGINNING of the Ancient Word, here in this place called Quiché. Here we shall inscribe, we shall implant the Ancient Word, the potential and source for everything done in the citadel of Quiché, in the nation of Quiché people.

And here we shall take up the demonstration, revelation, and account of how things were put in shadow and brought to light . . .

This is the account, here it is:

Now it still ripples, now it still murmurs, ripples, it still sighs, still hums, and it is empty under the sky.

Here follow the first words, the first eloquence:

There is not yet one person, one animal, bird, fish, crab, tree, rock, hollow, canyon, meadow, forest. Only the sky alone is there; the face of the earth is not clear. Only the sea alone

ABOVE: *The Sovereign Plumed Serpent,* K. Taube (1957–) from the Dresden Codex. Here he is shown seated, holding a snake in his hand. On his back he wears a quetzal bird, with its head behind his, its wings at the level of his shoulders, and its tail hanging down to the ground.
OPPOSITE: *Resplendent Quetzal,* E. Gould (1804–1841), England

is pooled under all the sky; there is nothing whatever gathered together. It is at rest; not a single thing stirs. It is held back, kept at rest under the sky.

Whatever there is that might be is simply not there: only the pooled water, only the calm sea, only it alone is pooled.

Whatever might be is simply not there: only murmurs, ripples, in the dark, in the night. Only the Maker, Modeler alone, Sovereign Plumed Serpent, the Bearers, Begetters are in the water, a glittering light. They are there, they are enclosed in quetzal feathers, in blue-green.

Thus the name, "Plumed Serpent." They are great knowers, great thinkers in their very being.

And of course there is the sky, and there is also the Heart of Sky. This is the name of the god, as it is spoken.

And then came his word, he came here to the Sovereign Plumed Serpent, here in the blackness, in the early dawn. He spoke with the Sovereign Plumed Serpent, and they talked, then they thought, then they worried. They agreed with each other, they joined their words, their thoughts. Then it was clear, then they reached accord in the light, and then humanity was clear, when they conceived the growth, the generation of trees, of bushes, and the growth of life, of humankind, in the blackness, in the early dawn, all because of the Heart of Sky, named Hurricane. Thunderbolt Hurricane comes first, the second is Newborn Thunderbolt, and the third is Sudden Thunderbolt.

So there were three of them, as Heart of Sky, who came to the Sovereign Plumed Serpent, when the dawn of life was conceived:

"How should the sowing be, and the dawning? Who is to be the provider, nurturer?"

"Let it be this way, think about it: this water should be removed, emptied out for the formation of the earth's own plate and platform, then should come the sowing, the dawning of the sky-earth. But there will be no high days and no bright praise for our work, our design, until the rise of the human work, the human design," they said.

And then the earth arose because of them, it was simply their word that brought it forth. For the forming of the earth they said "Earth." It arose suddenly, just like a cloud, like a mist, now forming, unfolding. Then the mountains were separated from the water, all at once the great mountains came forth. By their genius alone, by their cutting edge alone they carried out the conception of the mountain-plain, whose face grew instant groves of cypress and pine.

And the Plumed Serpent was pleased with this:

"It was good that you came, Heart of Sky, Hurricane, and Newborn Thunderbolt, Sudden Thunderbolt. Our work, our design will turn out well," they said.

And the earth was formed first, the mountain-plain. The channels of water were separated; their branches wound their ways among the mountains. The waters were divided when the great mountains appeared.

Such was the formation of the earth when it was brought forth by the Heart of Sky, Heart of Earth, as they are called, since they were the first to think of it. The sky was set apart, and the earth was set apart in the midst of the waters.

Such was their plan when they thought, when they worried about the completion of their work.

Traditional Mayan text
in Tedlock, *Popul Vuh*

THE ARCHAEOPTERYX'S SONG

I am only half out of this rock of scales.
What good is armour when you want to fly?
My tail is like a stony pedestal
and not a rudder. If I sit back on it
I sniff winds, clouds, rains, fogs where
I'd be, where I'd be flying, be flying high.
Dinosaurs are spicks and
all I see when I look back
is tardy turdy bonehead swamps
whose scruples are dumb tons.
Damnable plates and plaques
can't even keep out ticks.
They think when they make the ground thunder
as they lumber for a horn-lock or a rut
that someone is afraid, that everyone is afraid,
but no one is afraid. The lords of creation
are in my mate's next egg's next egg's next egg,

stegosaur. It's feathers I need, more feathers
for the life to come. And these iron teeth
I want away, and a smooth beak
to cut the air. And these claws
on my wings, what use are they
except to drag me down, do you imagine
I am ever going to crawl again?
When I first left that crag
and flapped low and heavy over the ravine
I saw past present and future
like a dying tyrannosaur
and skimmed it with a hiss.
I will teach my sons and daughters to live
on mist and fire and fly to the stars.

EDWIN MORGAN (1920–), Scotland

Owl made from narwhal vertebra, Inuit folk art,
artist unknown (contemporary)

Moving Toward the Ancient Bird

. . . LET US, BEFORE LEAVING the subject, once more look back across that awesome gulf of 150 million years to the days when *Archaeopteryx* hopped about on the shores of the reedy pools in Bavaria. It is hard to conceive of so long a time. The mind does not comprehend it. Imagine a line 150 feet long, each foot representing a million years; ourselves a point at this end, *Archaeopteryx* a point at the other. If we start moving toward the ancient bird, we shall find that by the time we have passed the days of Tutankhamen's great grandfather, we shall have progressed a distance about equal to the width of a thick pencil-line, or one millimeter to 3333 years. After going back the vast space of a third of an inch we shall have passed far beyond historic times to the early Stone Age of Man, and at the end of an inch we shall be well into Glacial times. The first foot of our 150-foot journey will have brought us only to the beginning of the latest or Pleistocene epoch of earth's history, and we will have accomplished less than half the journey ere we reach the fauna of the Paris Basin and the great *Diatryma* of Eocene days. And even when we at length reach the journey's end, we are still a long way from the starting point of birds. Thus we may realize that geologically speaking a thousand years is not really such a very long time; it is only that our thoughts are small.

GLOVER MORRILL ALLEN (1879–1942), United States
from *Birds and Their Attributes*

Goatsucker, M. Catesby (1679–1749), England

For a bird of the air shall carry the voice,
and that which hath wings shall tell the truth.

ECCLESIASTES X.20

III ~

DEATH COMES
AS A ROOSTER

Folk tales and parables

Winter, T. van Hoytema (1863–1917), Netherlands

POPULAR EXAMPLES OF FOLKLORIC BIRDS are everywhere: Woody Woodpecker with his maniacal laugh, Scrooge McDuck, Christopher Robin's Wise Old Owl, Big Bird of *Sesame Street*, and Harry Potter's messenger owl Hedwig.

Animals acting out versions of human strength or folly have always compelled and entertained us. Enigmatic animal spirits preceded our anthropomorphic gods: earlier generations lived in close and often dangerous proximity to wild animals, and were keenly vulnerable to the vagaries of the hunt. It isn't surprising that they created stories about these creatures, and in doing so strove to identify with them.

In *Diet of Souls*, John Houston's documentary on traditional Inuit hunting, there's a compelling exploration of how animism lingers on in the North. If you believe, as the Inuit have traditionally done, that the animals you must kill also have souls, and that their spirits are sometimes stronger than your own, then spiritual life is dangerous, and inescapably tragic.

We are far from that truth now. Most city children will never see a live sheep or cow. Nevertheless our tradition of animal stories still carries with it secularized echoes of magic, of shamanism—of a time when spirits moved between human and animal bodies; and when people believed (as some still do) that all living things have souls, and that we must learn from them.

For much of the seventies I lived and worked on a small farm north of Toronto. Among our collection of animals was a desperately earnest rooster, who protected and serviced about two dozen hens. The poor devil took his responsibilities so seriously that when I was feeding his flock or collecting their eggs I had to protect my legs by fending the rooster off with a tennis racquet. Moreover I don't think I ever broke open an egg that hadn't been fertilized.

Should a strange dog bark or a crow sail over the barnyard the rooster would explode into action, chasing his startled harem into the barn, all the while screaming havoc. Had he worked in the city he would have been recognized as a classic Type A personality.

One fateful day in spring, several threatening events occurred simultaneously. The sheep barged into the rooster's flock, separating it into two groups of hens. The rooster was trying to round them up when I appeared in the doorway with a shovel over my shoulder. Then I walked between the bird and his charges. It was all too much for the rooster. He uttered a series of frightful screams and then pitched over on his side. He was dead.

Before redeeming the unfortunate creature as coq au vin I showed the body to our veterinarian, to rule out some ghastly avian sickness. Contemplating the rooster's swollen, blood-filled head and neck, the vet said: "This bird died of rage." It certainly looked that way. I'd seen such faces glaring out from cars during rush hour, and recognized the symptoms.

What was the lesson? Nothing the bird intended to teach me. In folk tales and parables, the bird is our ventriloquist's dummy: the voice we hear is our own.

G.G.

Death Comes as a Rooster

A woman's husband was sick in bed. She did nothing but take care of the man, and every chance she got she prayed to the Lord, "Dear God, don't take him first. Let Death come first for me."

She repeated it constantly. Her compadre overheard her and said, "You'll know Death when you see him, compadre. He comes as a plucked rooster."

The woman kept on, begging Death, "Don't take my poor husband, take me instead."

Then the compadre caught a rooster, plucked its feathers, and put it out in the sun until it was crazed. When he turned it loose, it ran screeching into the sickroom. The wife took one look and said, "My God, it's Death!" She jumped behind the door and pointed her finger at her husband. "Over that way," she said. "The sick man is in the bed."

Traditional Cuban folktale
in Bierhorst, *Latin American Folktales*

ABOVE: Day of the Dead papier mâché folk art, artist unknown (contemporary)
OPPOSITE: *I Said Good Morning to the Rooster,* C. Pachter (1942–), Canada

THE CHOUGH

The chough, said a dictionary,
Is a relation of the raven
And a relative of the crow.
It's nearly extinct,
But lingers yet
In the forests about Oporto.
So read I as a little child
And saw a young Chough in its nest,
Its very yellow beak already tasting
The delicious eyes
Of missionaries and dead soldiers;
Its wicked mind already thinking
Of how it would line its frowsy nest
With the gold fillings of dead men's teeth.
When I grew older I learned
That the chough, the raven and the crow
That rise like a key signature of black sharps
In the staves and music of a scarlet sunset
Are not to be feared so much
As that carrion bird, within the brain,
Whose name is Devouring Years,
Who gobbles up and rends
All odds and ends
Of memory, good thoughts and recollections
That one has stored up between one's ears
And whose feet come out round either eye.

JAMES REANEY (1926–), Canada

Chough, F.O. Morris
(1810–1893), Ireland/England

VULTURE

A VULTURE IS THOUGHT TO BE named after its slow flying ("a volatu tardo"). Because of the great size of its body it certainly does not have rapidity of flight. Vultures, like eagles far above the sea, can discern corpses. By flying very high they can of course espy from up there many things which are otherwise obstructed from sight by the darkness of mountains. They say that vultures do not indulge in coition, and do not come together as pairs do in normal conjugal coupling, and that they therefore conceive without the seed of any male and they breed without mating. Offspring born to them proceed to very long lives, and they are given to life-spans of as much as a hundred years, and fate does not easily catch them out with premature deaths. *Spiritualiter:* What can they say, those who are accustomed to ridiculing our priests when they hear that a virgin conceived, and who think that an unmarried girl giving birth is impossible when her modesty had traditionally been defiled by no man? They consider impossible for the mother of God what is not denied as possible for vultures. A bird gives birth without a male, but when the betrothed Virgin Mary herself gives birth, they question her modesty. Surely we should observe that the Lord, who was born of her,

will affirm the truth? Vultures are accustomed to foretell the death of people by certain signs. On this evidence certain people are taught and instructed and, when they are preparing for a lamentable war between themselves and an opposing army, many of the said birds may follow the troops and indicate to them that large numbers of people are to fall in the battle and to become food for the vultures.

PETERBOROUGH BESTIARY

Vulture, Peterborough Bestiary MS53 (early 14th century)

from The Eye of the Albatross

. . . ON A CIRCUMNAVIGATING VOYAGE between 1719 and 1722, George Shelvocke was impressed by "the largest sort of sea-fowls . . . extending their wings 12 or 13 foot," and he called them "Albitroses."

Shelvocke's journal described a storm near Cape Horn, during which a "disconsolate" black albatross "accompanied us for several days, hovering about us as if he had lost himself." One of Shelvocke's officers, "observing, in one of his melancholy fits, that this bird was always hovering near us, imagined, from his colour, that it might be some ill omen. . . . The more to encourage his superstition, was the continued series of contrary tempestuous winds, which had oppress'd us ever since we had got into this sea." The man shot the albatross, "not doubting (perhaps) that we should have a fair wind after it." What actually followed were winds so severe it took them six weeks to sight the coast of Chile. By the late 1760s, Captain Cook's naturalist Joseph Banks began using the modern form *albatross*, and this word, with its Greek and Arabic roots, is now understood worldwide.

Dusky Albatross (detail), J.J. Audubon (1785–1851), France / United States

In 1797 William Wordsworth had been reading Shelvocke's account when he took a long, moonlit night walk with Samuel Taylor Coleridge. During their passage on moorland paths from Alfoxden to the fishing village of Watchet, Wordsworth described the incident to Coleridge, thus providing the seed of inspiration that in 1798 blossomed into "The Rime of the Ancient Mariner." That epic poem gave us, of course, the image of the albatross around one's neck. Any belief among seamen that killing albatrosses would bring bad luck dates from Coleridge's poem. (A more genuine notion actually borne by some mariners—if perhaps tongue in cheek—was that when old sailors died they returned as albatrosses.)

Coleridge's poem turned the albatross into a metaphor from which the bird has never escaped. But the metaphor has been distorted and is often misapplied. "An albatross" has become an icon of unshakably burdensome responsibility, psychological distress, or social baggage. We hear people say things like "That project has been an albatross around her neck." Somehow the albatross has been made the villain, the bad thing. But an albatross is not the same as a white elephant (some physical thing too big to manage and that no one else wants, like a huge, inherited run-down house that won't sell) or a ball and chain (an acquired burden that is a constant emotional drag). Only if the dilemma you have is your own fault, if your suffering is deserved, is it, metaphorically speaking, your "albatross." In the original poem, the crewman is made to wear around his neck the albatross he killed. The burden of his own deed is his just punishment and reminder for his offense.

And I had done a hellish thing
And it would work 'em woe:
For all averred, I had killed the bird
That made the breeze to blow.

In the windless calm that follows, the sailing ship lies helplessly stranded under "a hot and copper sky," beneath "the bloody Sun." Eventually afflicted by horrible thirst— "Water, water, every where, / Nor any drop to drink. . . . / And every tongue, through utter drought, / Was withered at the root. . . . / With throats unslaked, with black lips baked, / We could nor laugh nor wail"—everyone on the ship, except the Mariner, dies. Thus by its authorship of the wind the bird plays a critical role in atmospheric nature and human survival, which is unrecognized and unappreciated until the bird is killed, whereupon all share the unforeseen consequence of its destruction.

CARL SAFINA (1955–), United States

He Cheated the Bird

FROM THE VEHICLE I was unloading I watched Cheruyiot, tall, lithe, and fine-boned as are so many East Africans, moving with the long elastic step of a born plainsman between the Land-Rovers and the kitchen that John and Jeremiah were making near by. Although he did not speak a word of their language the three of them appeared old friends. As he put down a can of water Jeremiah looked up with a smile and said precisely, in English: 'Thank you, Jambo,' the nickname they had given him after the Swahili greeting he had used on their first meeting. I watched him and John go off into the bush and come back dragging branches of dead wood until a pile high enough for a pagan king's pyre was stacked handy for Jeremiah.

Fantastical Bird, Sarah Webster (1976–), Canada

'Thank you, John! Thank you, Jambo!' Jeremiah said again, the laugh that went with it quickly giving way to that dedicated look which comes upon a man's face when he makes a fire in a natural place. For one brief instant between the striking of the match and the quick leap of the first flame upwards on a pigs-tail of startled smoke, Jeremiah's bowed head might have been that of the first man lighting his first fire. Miraculously, just at that moment a little bird appeared on the branch of a tree behind him, flapping its wings and delivering with a silver clarity the urgent message my Bushman nurses had decoded for me as a child: 'Quick! Quick! Honey! Quick!'

At once Jeremiah stood up from his fire in amazement, and then a laugh straight from the pit of his stomach and round with content, broke from him.

'Look, Master!', he called, the marvel deep in his voice. 'Look, John! Look, Jambo! The honey-diviner.'

He took a step forward as if prepared to drop everything and follow the bird to the store of wild honey it was so ardently advertising. The little bird saw his step and fluttered hopefully on to a tree deeper in the bush.

I smiled at Jeremiah, shook my head and said: 'It's too late!'

Soon the unfollowed bird was back again on its perch by the fire and stayed there beseeching Jeremiah with the hysteria of despair, until the sun red and tired sank into the leaves of the dense trees.

'That, John, that, Jambo,' I heard Jeremiah lecturing them in his pedantic way as he busied himself about his pots, 'is the honey-diviner of my country, which, I'll have you know, lies just on the other side of that river which goes like a great wind through these trees. . . . Follow the bird and it will lead you to sweet brown honey but always be careful to share the honey with it. . . . If you do not, it will punish you heavily. . . . I once knew a man whose stomach was too big for his eyes—no, not a man of my own people but of the stupid Bapedi—he cheated the bird out of its share and the very next day it called on him again and led him straight to a hole where there was no honey but an angry female puff-adder who bit him on his greedy hand and killed him. . . . Another bird who had been cheated once led a man into the mouth of a lion . . . I tell you that bird is too clever for a man to cheat.'

Clever was Jeremiah's favourite adjective of praise.

'Auck!' exclaimed John who had understood it all and laughed out of politeness as well as wonder. But Cheruyiot who caught only the gist of the meaning from the ono-matopoeic words and expressive gestures just showed his white teeth and pointed with his finger appreciatively at the bird.

'Look, Jambo!' Jeremiah told him demonstrating his meaning on his own thumb. 'If you must point in that direc-tion, please be so good as to refrain from doing it so rudely with your finger straight out like that, but instead, politely, only with the knuckle of your thumb, the tip turned down towards your hand thus. . . . Otherwise you'll send away the rain we'll be needing soon.'

LAURENS VAN DER POST (1906–1996), South Africa from *The Lost World of the Kalahari*

TALE LXVIII.
OF MAINTAINING TRUTH TO THE LAST

IN THE REIGN OF GORDIAN, there was a certain noble soldier who had a fair but vicious wife. It happened that her husband having occasion to travel, the lady sent for her gallant. Now, one of her handmaids, it seems, was skilful in interpreting the song of birds; and in the court of the castle there were three cocks. During the night, while the gallant was with his mistress, the first cock began to crow. The lady heard it, and said to her servant, "Dear friend, what says yonder cock?" She replied, "That you are grossly injuring your husband." "Then," said the lady, "kill that cock without delay." They did so; but soon after the second cock crew, and the lady repeated her question. "Madam," said the handmaid, "he says 'My companion died for revealing the truth, and for the same cause, I am prepared to die.'" "Kill him," cried the lady,— which they did. After this, the third cock crew. "What says he?" asked she again. "Hear, see, and say nothing, if you would live in peace." "Oh, oh!" said the lady, "don't kill him." And her orders were obeyed.

My beloved, the emperor is God; the soldier, Christ; and the wife, the soul. The gallant is the devil. The handmaid is conscience. The first cock is our Saviour, who was put to death; the second is the martyrs; and the third is a preacher who ought to be earnest in declaring the truth, but, being deterred by menaces, is afraid to utter it.

Traditional Latin (Medieval) story
in Swan and Hooper, *Gesta Romanorum*

Zen and the Birds of Appetite

Where there is carrion lying, meat-eating birds circle and descend. Life and death are two. The living attack the dead, to their own profit. The dead lose nothing by it. They gain too, by being disposed of. Or they seem to, if you must think in terms of gain and loss. Do you then approach the study of Zen with the idea that there is something to be gained by it? This question is not intended as an implicit accusation. But it is, nevertheless, a serious question. Where there is a lot of fuss about "spirituality," "enlightenment" or just "turning on," it is often because there are buzzards hovering around a corpse. This hovering, this circling, this descending, this celebration of victory, are not what is meant by the study of Zen—even though they may be a highly useful exercise in other contexts. And they enrich the birds of appetite.

Zen enriches no one. There is no body to be found. The birds may come and circle for a while in the place where it is thought to be. But they soon go elsewhere. When they are gone, the "nothing," the "no-body" that was there, suddenly appears. That is Zen. It was there all the time but the scavengers missed it, because it was not their kind of prey.

Thomas Merton (1915–1968), France/United States

Californian Turkey Vulture, J.J. Audubon (1785–1851), France/United States

Californian Turkey Vulture.

Drawn from Nature by J.J.Audubon, F.R.S. F.L.S.   Lithd Printed & Cold by J.T.Bowen, Philad.ª

THE WEE BIRD

THE STORY'S ABOUT A LITTLE GIRL. It was one fine day, her mother sent her for a joog of milk to the dairy. So she says, 'Can I take ma skippin-rope with me?'

Her mother was awful bad, says, 'No, ye can't,' she says.

'But I won't spill the milk, Mummy, I promise.'

'Well,' her mother says, 'ye can take the skippin-rope, but if ye spill the milk, I'll kill you.'

So the little girl takes the skippin-rope, an on the way goin, she's skippin with it, an she gits the milk, an she's skippin away, comin back, the milk in the jug, an the jug falls an breaks, so she looks fir anither jug. So this kind old lady comes along, says, 'I've got a jug, jist the neighbour of the one you broke.' She gies it to the little girl, an the little girl goes back fir more milk. So when she goes back fir more milk, she doesn't skip on the way comin home, she folds the rope up an then carries it in her hand.

When she comes home, her mummy says, 'Well, did ye get the milk?'

She says, 'Yes, Mummy.'

Blue Tit, K. Svolinsky (1896–1986), Czech

She says, 'Let me see the jug,' an she looked at the jug, she says, 'This isn't my jug.' She says, 'This is a different jug.'

She says, 'No, it's no, Mummy,' she says, 'that's the same jug as ye give me.'

She says, 'No, it's not. It's a different jug,' she says. 'My jug had a blue stripe on the top. This one has a red.'

So her mummy killed her, an baked her in a pie. But then her father comes in. He asked where the little girl wes, an the woman said, 'She'll likely be out playin.'

Says, 'Well, hurry up an shout her for her dinner.'

She says, 'Ach! Let the child play.' So she gives the man his dinner, an when he eats hauf-way through the pie, he sees this finger in it, an it had a little silver ring on it, an he looks at it an says, 'Why! This is my daughter's ring,' he says. 'What did ye do to her?'

She says, 'Well, I told her that if she broke my jug, I wad kill her, so I've killed her.'

'Now,' he says, 'look at what ye've went an done.' Says, 'I've a good mind to kill you.' Says, 'No,' he says, 'I'll let ye live.'

The two sons cam in an they were lookin fir thir sister, an the father told them whit had happened. So they startit to cry.

But then, Christmas came, an this wee little bird wes always peeping through the window. So when the boys put crumbs an things out to the window, the little bird ett it. Bit then it wes Christmas night, time fir to get the presents, then a voice cam doon the chimney: 'Brother, brother, look up, look up, look up an see what I've got.' So when the brother looked up, she dropped down a bagful of toys and sweets.

Then she said it again, an the other brother looked up, an she dropped don anither bag full of toys an sweets.

Then she says, 'Father, father, look up, look up, an see

what I've got.' So when the father looked up, she dropped the father a new suit an a letter, an on the envelope it said, 'Don't open this letter until two hours after Christmas night.'

So she shouted, 'Mother, mother, look up, look up an see what I've got,' an when the mother looked up, she dropped a stone, an hit the mother on the head. Killed her.

So when the two hours came, the father opened up the letter, an he read it, he says, 'Dear Father, this is your little daughter. The spell is broken. Once I have killed my mother, I shall come back to you on New Year's Eve.'

So New Year's Eve come, an they're waitin an waitin, waitin fir the daughter to come. Bit she didn't come, an then, three minutes before midnight, a knock came on the window. They open't the window, the little bird came in, says, 'I'm home, Father.'

The father says, 'Why!' he says, 'You're the little bird now!'

She says, 'I know, but if you take my mother's ring pinkie, pinkie of the right hand,' she says, 'I'll come back tae a girl.'

So he goes away to where the mother was buried an takes the right pinkie, where still the ring wes, the same as on her. He took it, an the little girl changed back from a bird into a girl. When she took the ring, she says, 'My mother weren't really bad, it wes jist that the Devil was inside her,' she says, 'bit now that she's gone,' she says, 'she'll be in Heaven.' An she took the ring that wes on her own pinkie, she put the two in a box, an they all lived happily iver after.

Traditional Scottish tale
in Bruford and MacDonald, *Scottish Traditional Tales*

FROM THE METAMORPHOSES

WITH THESE WORDS Calliope, the oldest of our sisterhood, ended her song, the song I have just recited. The nymphs agreed unanimously that the goddesses of Helicon were the victors. Our defeated opponents replied by hurling abuse at us, until I exclaimed: "So, it is not enough that you have deserved punishment by forcing this contest, but you add insult to injury? Our patience is not unlimited: we shall follow where our anger prompts, and proceed to punish you." The Macedonian women laughed and scorned my threats, but as they tried to speak, menacing us with loud cries and wanton gestures, they saw feathers sprouting from their nails and

plumage covering their arms. They looked at each other, watching their faces narrow into horny beaks, as a new addition was made to the birds of the forest. When they tried to beat their breasts, the movement of their arms raised them, to hover in the air. They had become magpies, the scandalmongers of the woods. Even now, as birds, they still retain their original power of speech. They still chatter harshly and have an insatiable desire to talk.

Ovid (43bc–ad17)

Magpie, K. Svolinsky (1896–1986), Czech

The Finch in May

ONCE IN THE OLD, old days there was a finch that had been wise enough to nest in the linden tree of a convent.

Wise enough? No doubt the idea was an inspiration from on high. God watches over all things, even the life of a finch.

Providence wakes each morning
An hour or two before the sun.

So there's the finch in its tree, among the new May leaves. It was May, you know, Mary's month, when narcissus bloom in the high meadows—the flowers they call the white gloves of Our Lady. Eight times a day, from its nest in the middle of the cloister, the finch heard the nuns at their prayers, and from prime to terce to compline the same two words kept coming

Serin, F.O. Morris (1810–1893), Ireland/England

back. It heard them, listened, then tried them out with its own little bird throat. The dear thing didn't know it was an angel from Heaven who'd brought those two words down to mankind when he came to proclaim our salvation. The leaves swayed, and the sunbeams through them swung like censers. There in the green, moving light and the gentle breezes, the finch repeated over and over those two words: *Ave Maria, Ave Maria!*

The convent stood under steep, forested slopes and towering spires of rock, beneath a spur of the mountains. One evening the finch had ventured up into those piney, stony wilds when suddenly it felt a presence hovering above it, under the clouds. With all the speed of its wings it fled for the convent roof and home.

But a kite's eyes are more piercing than hell. The one slowly circling up there, round and round in the streaming clouds and wind, stopped like a spider hanging from its thread. The white bands on the finch's wings had given it away.

The kite dropped and gripped the finch in its talons.

Nearly fainting, the little bird cried out. It cried out the two words that had so gotten into its head that it had said them over and over all day long: *Ave Maria, Ave Maria.*

So great is the power of Mary's name that the name alone—just one call to Our Lady—loosened the kite's grip. Up again into the clouds it flew, not daring now to touch its prey.

The terrified finch raced and dove straight into the heart of its linden tree. Among the sweet flowers again, saved, comforted, and overjoyed, it fairly nestled into her hands who is the Flower and Queen of the World.

Traditional French folktale
in Pourrat, *French Folktales*

THE PETRELS

Believing only in what can't be done,
We have taken as our target
The blood-red disc of the sun!

THE FIRST THING that has to be said is that petrels are short-sighted birds. To this congenital infirmity may be attributed their uncertain flight and their shy, yet incautious, behaviour. The fact that their very habitat is blurred and unsatisfactorily lit may perhaps explain (although not excuse) the incongruous adventure into which they so senselessly rushed one day.

It might have been seven in the evening. The petrels were sitting on the warm sand of a lonely beach, along the line of foam which the tide leaves, before turning, to mark the territory it imagines it has conquered. A man out after gulls with his dog would have taken them, from a distance, for a row of white stones among the flotsam. A few jellyfish still caught the light here and there; a pool reflected a cloud; a ship seemed motionless on the horizon.

Finally, like a great blinding moon, the sun (it shines for everyone, alas) was making ready to fall into the water in front of all the usual promenaders of the coasts watching for the last green ray.

But the petrels knew how much deeper the night is for them than for other birds, and they were filled with sadness. One of them stood, stretched its neck skyward and voiced a brief lament. Hearing the signal, the others silently flapped their wings, still on the ground, as if to blow the dark away.

Leach's Petrel, J.J. Audubon (1785–1851), France/United States

This was an ancient custom, a relic from superstitious times, like a religion they no longer believed in. The ritual over, the petrels should have been thinking, as they did every evening, about settling on one leg and going off to sleep, forgetting the day just done in the certainty of another, just the same, tomorrow. Not one, not even among the oldest, was wise enough to set the example. They could not take their eyes off the sun, which was taking an eternity over all the elaborate ceremonial prescribed for its setting.

Suddenly, like the restlessness which sometimes drives whole tribes to migrate, an irrational urge set them running, every one, clumsily down the beach to the sea. Then every wing opened, and they all took flight, unsteadily over the first few waves, but soon in a perfect triangle, and through the air they sped, wings beating the rhythm of a sailors' song, straight for the last dazzling signs of light; over the inshore line of reefs that rise and sink with each slow heave of the sea; past a small fishing boat returning to port, barely heeling in the wind, one side red, the other dusk-black. All along the coast, one by one, the lighthouses were blinking into life.

At first, the petrels skimmed along on wings which long ago, 'like those of all sea-birds', took on the shape of the waves. Herds of white horses from the open sea galloped frantically beneath them. A gull, soaring high, wheeled unconcernedly against the sky before flying off, uncomprehending. Porpoises leapt from the water in hopeful imitation of Arion's dolphins, and followed the birds for a while, trying to guess what quarry could be tempting them so far or what danger could be causing them such fright. But (as has often been regretted) the petrels never met the cormorant of good counsel, who would have told them in his wisdom: 'You short-sighted birds, how little you know the world! Go back home and go to sleep! A sun once gone is never caught.'

They flew up to the furthest reaches of space, so high that the Ocean looks curved and at peace. Up there, in the night, the western horizon still has a pallor which marks it apart from every other. They flew through the gathering dark in a white gust of wings and cries. It is even said that they accidentally holed a cloud which had lost its fellows and was waiting till daylight to resume its trek across the seas. But soon they found themselves locked into a hemisphere of unbroken night, tinged only by the frosty geometry of far-distant stars. They had to sing louder then, to sustain their faith, for there was no longer the slightest trace of light to guide it.

Some, exhausted at last, would suddenly fold their wings and plummet headlong from the flock. Beads of blood dripped from beaks and blew in a spray in the wind. Every bird was buffeted and rumpled, and it is said that it snowed feathers on the sea that night. Nothing could dash the head-strong hope of that ignorant, dim-witted breed.

Those few who apparently survived the adventure have never been able to understand how they could have been chasing the sun since it set and still have it come up behind them. And so, today, the reputation of the petrel is firmly established.

Often, on a stormy night, they will crash head-first into the dazzle of a lighthouse.

JEAN DE LA VILLE DE MIRMONT (1886–1914), France

Fasting for the Hand
of the Queen's Daughter

Bru Pigeon and Bru Owl both fell in love with the queen's daughter. Though they had been friends, they had a big fight over who would win her hand, and they decided that they would have a contest. So they went to the king and told him their problem, and he said that they must have a contest over who could stay hungry the longest from Monday to Friday.

So they went into the bush; the pigeon sat in a berry and the owl in a dry tree. When Monday came, Bru Pigeon started in singing:

This day is Monday morning,

Tama tama tam.

And Bru Owl answered:

Whoo-oo tama tama tam.

Meanwhile, Bru Pigeon, when no one could see him at night, sneaked down from the branch he was perched on and ate a few berries and in the morning he drank from the dew that fell on the branch. Since Owl didn't have anything growing like this in his tree, he couldn't even think of pulling such a trick. And there were no mice and other such vermin scampering around on those branches either, the things he likes to eat most.

So Tuesday morning came, and Bru Pigeon started singing his boasting song again just as loudly:

This day is Tuesday morning,

Tama tama tam.

And Bru Owl answered:

Whoo-oo tama tama tam.

Now Wednesday and then Thursday and Friday mornings came around, and still Bru Pigeon kept singing the same verses. Now Bru Owl was really getting hungry. Bru Pigeon was eating berries all this time and drinking the water from the morning dew.

When Friday came, Bru Pigeon started in to sing again:

This day is Friday morning,

Tama tama tam.

But by now Bru Owl had gotten weaker and weaker. He could hardly answer. So when Saturday came and Bru Pigeon started in on his song; he didn't hear any voice in reply at all.

When Bru Pigeon heard no boast coming back at him, he flew over to the tree where Bru Owl was and found Bru Owl was stiff dead. Bru Pigeon took Bru Owl on his shoulder and carried him to the king, and lay Bru Owl down at the king's feet. And by that he won the hand of the queen and king's daughter.

They live in peace, they die in peace, they were buried in a pot of candle grease.

Traditional Bahamian folktale
in Abrahams, *Afro-American Folktales*

One for the pigeon, one for the crow,
one to rot, and one to grow.

TRADITIONAL SOWING PROVERB

IV ~

ODIN'S RAVENS

Bird companions

Kakura (Garuda), one of the Eight Guardians of Buddhism,
housed in the Kofuku-ji Temple, Nara, Japan

THE NORSE GOD ODIN, the All-father, had two ravens, one named Thought (Huginn) and the other Memory (Muninn). Each day they flew about the world, and on returning told the god what they had seen. Much of Odin's power is attributed to his "raven knowledge," as second sight is called in parts of Scotland. Perhaps it is this kind of belief that survives in the folk saying, "A little bird told me."

There are good reasons why Raven became an iconic figure. These birds cannot open large carcasses, especially frozen ones; they must therefore follow hunting carnivores, such as wolves, bears and humans, who will do the hard work for them. For millennia early humans hunted in family groups, just as wolves do. Field researchers in New England told Bernd Heinrich[1] that hunting wolves are almost always accompanied by a raven or two. Ravens must have associated with human hunters in the same way. Indeed they often still do, during moose and deer hunting seasons.

Ravens, or "wolf birds" as they are sometimes called, not only follow hunting carnivores; there's good reason to believe they actually collaborate, by leading them to prey. Ravens are very intelligent birds; as they are capable of spotting quarry from far above their

1. author of *Ravens in Winter* and *The Mind of the Raven*

earthbound partners, it's likely that, over the long years, they figured out a way of bringing predator and prey together. Heinrich describes older Inuit hunters who insist that Raven has been an active partner in their hunts.

Ravens aren't the only birds capable of choosing to relate to humans. Parrots are also high on the list. Early in the autumn of 1964 I bought a parrot in Oaxaca, Mexico. He was a handsome creature, very healthy and full of life. I named him Harold Wilson. He scarcely said anything at all, but he barked like two dogs at once, made roaring noises like a vacuum cleaner, and spoke my sons' names. He was bright and affectionate, and soon became an amusing and responsive member of the family.

However, back in Toronto a year later I became increasingly uneasy about Harold's situation. As winter cold and darkness set in I saw that the bird was miserable: diminishing daylight must have been bad enough, but I also sensed that he was lonely.

By spring I'd arranged to give him to the Toronto Zoo, a modest operation back then. The director led us to the aviary himself, where a congenial cage had been prepared. Waiting inside was a female parrot named Olive.

Watched by my sons and a gathering crowd, I entered the cage, with Harold on my wrist. When I placed him on the main perch, Olive shuffled away. I said my goodbyes and turned to leave. Then Harold did something that astonished me. For the very first time, and in exactly the voice my kids might have used, he called out, "Daddy!" When I turned to look at him he was leaning toward me expectantly. "Daddy," he repeated.

I don't remember what I said to him. Something about him being happier there, that he'd soon make friends. The kind of things you say to kids when you abandon them at camp. But outside the aviary I could still hear him calling, "Daddy! Daddy!" as we walked away. I was shattered to discover that Harold knew my name, and that he did so because he'd identified himself with my children. I now believe he'd known it all along, but was using it—for the first time—out of desperation.

Both Konrad Lorenz and Bernd Heinrich mention instances of birds calling out the private names of intimates when threatened by serious danger. I am no longer surprised by such information. We think of our captive birds as our pets, but perhaps we are their pets, as well.

G.G.

Frigate Bird, J. White (c.1545–1593), England/United States

Folded in the Flag of Ahab

The harpoon was darted; the stricken whale flew forward; with igniting velocity the line ran through the grooves;—ran foul. Ahab stooped to clear it; he did clear it; but the flying turn caught him round the neck, and voicelessly as Turkish mutes bowstring their victim, he was shot out of the boat, ere the crew knew he was gone. Next instant, the heavy eye-splice in the rope's final end flew out of the stark-empty tub, knocked down an oarsman, and smiting the sea, disappeared in its depths.

For an instant, the tranced boat's crew stood still; then turned. "The ship? Great God, where is the ship?" Soon they through dim, bewildering mediums saw her sidelong fading phantom, as in the gaseous Fata Morgana; only the upper-most masts out of water; while fixed by infatuation, or fidelity, or fate, to their once lofty perches, the pagan harpooneers still maintained their sinking lookouts on the sea. And now, concentric circles seized the lone boat itself, and all its crew, and each floating oar, and every lance-pole, and spinning, animate and inanimate, all round and round in one vortex, carried the smallest chip of the Pequod out of sight.

But as the last whelmings intermixingly poured themselves over the sunken head of the Indian at the mainmast, leaving a few inches of the erect spar yet visible, together with long streaming yards of the flag, which calmly undulated, with ironical coincidings, over the destroying billows they almost touched;—at that instant, a red arm and a hammer hovered backwardly uplifted in the open air, in the act of nailing the flag faster and yet faster to the subsiding spar. A sky-hawk that tauntingly had followed the main-truck downwards from its natural home among the stars, pecking at the flag, and incommoding Tashtego there; this bird now chanced to intercept its broad fluttering wing between the hammer and the wood; and simultaneously feeling that etherial thrill, the submerged savage beneath, in his death-gasp, kept his hammer frozen there; and so the bird of heaven, with archangelic shrieks, and his imperial beak thrust upwards, and his whole captive form folded in the flag of Ahab, went down with his ship, which, like Satan, would not sink to hell till she had dragged a living part of heaven along with her, and helmeted herself with it.

Now small fowls flew screaming over the yet yawning gulf; a sullen white surf beat against its steep sides; then all collapsed, and the great shroud of the sea rolled on as it rolled five thousand years ago.

HERMAN MELVILLE (1819–1891), United States
from *Moby Dick*

GIRLS CAME STREAMING OVER THE SEA

LATE ONE AFTERNOON, just as the evening star flashed the signal of twilight, the girls came streaming over the sea toward the island.

At the first far-away glimpse, the men dropped their tools and ran to the water's edge. Honey Smith waded out, waist-deep.

"Well, what do you know about that?" he called out. "Pipe the formation!"

They came massed vertically. In the distance they might have been a rainbow torn from its moorings, borne violently forward on a high wind. The rainbow broke in spots, fluttered, and then came together again. It vibrated with color. It pulsed with iridescence.

"How the thunder—" Addington began and stopped. "Well, can you beat it?" he concluded.

The human column was so arranged that the wings of one of the air-girls concealed the body of another just above her.

The "dark one" led, flying low, her scarlet pinions beating slowly back and forth about her head.

Just above, near enough for her body to be concealed by the scarlet wings of the "dark one," but high enough for her pointed brown face to peer between their curves, came the "plain one."

Higher flew the "thin one." Her body was entirely covered by the orange wings of the "plain one," but her copper-colored hair made a gleamy spot in their vase-shaped opening.

Still higher appeared the "peachy one." She seemed to be holding her lustrous blonde head carefully centered in the

A Prayer to God, L.W. Hawkins (1849–1910), Germany / France

oval between the "thin one's" green-and-yellow plumage. She looked like a portrait in a frame.

Highest of them all, floating upright, a Winged Victory of the air, her silver wings towering straight above her head, the cameo face of the "quiet one" looked level into the distance.

Their wings moved in rotation, and with machine-like regularity. First one pair flashed up, swept back and down, then another, and another. As they neared, the color seemed the least wonderful detail of the picture. For it changed in effect from a column of glittering wings to a column of girl-faces, a column that floated light as thistle-down, a column that divided, parted, opened, closed again.

The background of all this was a veil of dark gauze at the horizon-line, its foil a golden, virgin moon, dangling a single brilliant star.

"They're talking!" Honey Smith exclaimed. "And they're leaving!"

The girls did not pause once. They flew in a straight line over the island to the west, always maintaining their columnar formation. At first the men thought that they were making for the trees. They ran after them. The speed of their running had no effect this time on their visitors, who continued to sail eastward. The men called on them to stay. They called repeatedly, singly and in chorus. They called in every tone of humble masculine entreaty and of arrogant masculine command. But their cries might have fallen on marble ears. The girls neither turned nor paused. They disappeared.

INEZ HAYNES GILMORE (1873–1970),
Brazil/United States
from *Angel Island*

VIRGIN AND NIGHTINGALE

The courting of a girl and boy
who love and sigh and touch and toy
inflames the nightingale with joy:
she has to trill and coo it.

She's love's announcer and town-crier;
she lights the spark and stokes the fire;
she swells the lover with desire,
then boasts that he'll pursue it.

I've heard her in a leafy glade
encouraging some heated blade
to pierce a girl who was a maid—
and countless times will rue it.

A lady may be made of stone,
her heart encased in bronze, not bone;
but when she hears this melting tone
her body burns to do it.

The nightingale takes Cupid's part;
When he's installed the teasing dart
She makes the inflammation start
By wanton warblings to it.

Traditional Latin (Medieval) poem
in Adcock, *The Virgin and the Nightingale*

1844: MEXICO CITY
THE WARRIOR COCKS

THE CHURCH, landlord and moneylender, possesses half of
Mexico. The other half belongs to a handful of gentlemen
and to Indians penned up in their communities. The proprietor of the presidency is General López de Santa Anna,
who watches over public peace and the good health of his
fighting cocks.

Santa Anna governs with a cock in his arms. Thus, he
receives bishops and ambassadors, and to tend to a wounded
cock he abandons cabinet meetings. He founds more cockfight arenas than hospitals and issues more cockfight rules
than decrees on education. Cockfighting men form his personal court, along with cardsharps and widows of colonels
who never were.

Cockfighting, Anglesey Hunt Mss.f.42

He is very fond of a piebald cock that pretends to be a female and flirts with the enemy, then after making a fool of him slashes him to death; but of them all he prefers the fierce Pedrito. He brought Pedrito from Veracruz with some soil too, so Pedrito could wallow in it without nostalgia. Santa Anna personally fixes the blade on the spur. He exchanges bets with muleteers and vagabonds, and chews feathers from the rival to give it bad luck. When he has no coins left, he throws medals into the cockpit.

"I'll give eight to five!"

"Eight to four if you like!"

A lightning flash pierces the whirl of feathers and Pedrito's spur tears out the eyes or opens the throat of any champion. Santa Anna dances on one leg and the killer raises his crest, beats his wings and sings.

Eduardo Galeano (1945–), Uruguay

FROM THE HERON

IT DIDN'T FALL AT ONCE. He saw it give a kind of jerk, up in the sky, flap its broad brown wings awkwardly, then veer toward the sandbar from which the shots had been fired. It struggled to keep aloft, to gain altitude. But then it let itself go, abruptly, and came down as if it were being broken into pieces. It really was an old Caproni, he had time to say to himself at the moment when it plunged to the water and sank—the kind of plane they used in the First World War, all canvas, wires, and wood.

He thought it was dead, and that the dog would burst out and collect it. But no: as soon as it surfaced, it pulled itself up on its stilt legs, moving here and there, in jerks, its minuscule head. "Where am I?" it seemed to be wondering. "And what's happened to me?"

It still hadn't realized anything: not a thing. Or so little, in any case, that though one wing, the right, hung limply along its side, it made a movement of its shoulder blades, at one point, as if preparing to take flight. Only then, evidently, it became aware it was wounded. And in fact, from that moment on, it gave up any further efforts of the kind.

Restless, never ceasing to turn the smooth, slightly foolish, viveur's head, prolonged behind the nape by the strange, almost imperceptible, filiform antenna, it still tried to get its bearings, to recognize, if not the places, at least the nature of the objects surrounding it. A few steps away, for example, it noticed the punt, half on land and half in the water. What was that? A boat, or perhaps the body of a great, sleeping animal? Best to keep out of its way, anyhow. Better not risk approaching the little beach of fine, compact sand where that dark, menacing thing lay crosswise: much better. The pain in its side, for that matter, could no longer be felt. If it just avoided moving its wing, it felt no pain. It could wait.

He looked at it, full of anxiety, identifying with it completely. For him, too, the reason of many things was obscure. Why had Gavino fired? And why didn't he stand up now, and fire a second shot, the *coup de grâce*? Wasn't this the rule? And the dog? What was he afraid of, Gavino: that the heron, not having lost enough blood, might use its beak to defend itself? And the heron? What would it do? Wait, yes: but for what, and how long? His head felt befuddled, stunned: crammed with questions that received no answer.

Many minutes went by like this. Until, suddenly, he realized that the heron had moved.

It was heading in his direction, he observed, after he had raised one hand to shield his eyes from the glistening of the water—right toward the hogshead. But it was obvious. The heron had seen the decoys. Colored as they were, and struck by the sun's sidelong rays, they naturally seemed a flock of real birds, busy feeding. It was worth trusting them. There was no danger, surely, around there.

It advanced, dragging its wing in the water, in little,

rapid, successive darts, punctuated by brief pauses, carefully choosing the most shallow stretches of water. It passed the decoys closely, came forward, farther forward. And finally he found it face to face, an arm's length from the hogshead, preparing to step ashore. Once again it had stopped. Brown all over, except for the feathers of the neck and breast, a delicate beige tone, and except for the legs, the yellow-brown of fleshless bone, of relics, it bent its head slightly to one side, observing him: curious, perhaps, but not frightened. And he, without moving, almost without breathing (it was bleeding from a hole halfway along the wing, at the joint), he was able to return, at some length, that gaze. . . .

It had huddled against the hogshead, now, just like a shivering old man, seeking the sun; and he could no longer see it, he sensed it. From time to time it shifted: looking for a better position, or to give itself a shake. Large, bony, disproportionate—and half crippled in the bargain—it judged its movements badly. It kept bumping into the hogshead.

For minutes and minutes, nevertheless, it stayed erect: perfectly immobile. In a careful, sideways position to the cold, whistling gusts of the sea wind, and with the warm planks of the hogshead behind it, what was it doing? It was a bit reassured, perhaps. Though, even now, it hadn't understood much; it still kept looking around. Regain strength: this, for the present, it must be saying to itself, was the chief aim. And once regained, whoosh, it would impetuously spread its wings and fly off.

More time went by: he didn't know how much.

Suddenly three shots in succession, followed by the same number of thuds, shook him painfully.

He turned his head toward Gavino.

"Isn't that enough?" he complained, in a low voice.

He waited until the birds surfaced (coots: all three still, dead), and looked at his watch.

Unfortunately It was only two o'clock; and this light, perfect for shooting, would last another hour and a half at least. And besides, even if he, personally, had had more than enough: could he, at this point, raise his arm and signal Gavino to stop? True, for a little while, the heron hadn't moved at all. If it was still alive, though, what could they do with it? Finish it off with a gun, point-blank? No: that was out. Capture it then? Lean out of the hogshead, pick it up, in his arms, and then take it to the city? How? In the car? And then, where could he keep it? In a cage down in the courtyard? He could imagine Nives, if she saw him come home with a bird like this, and, what's more, wounded, a bird which in veterinarian's fees alone would cost God knows what. He could imagine her shouts, her protests, her whining. . . .

The dog had barely finished coming and going. She had collected the last coot, brought it dutifully to the proper person. And then, turning by chance to the right, toward the strip of land, as if to seek, from that direction, some kind of suggestion, he saw again the heron.

It had already moved about ten yards away from the hogshead, and, from the direction it had taken, it seemed to want to reach that strip of land. The racket of the shooting just now had surely frightened it. Then it had seen the dog go and come three times in a row, returning to shore each time with a coot in her mouth; and, though wounded, though weakened by loss of blood, and consequently more anxious than ever to enjoy there, sheltered from the wind, the last warmth of the sun, at a certain moment it had thought that it was wise still, immediately, to "move on." The long strip of land, over there, thickly covered with vegetation, more or less the same color as its feathers, and mostly tall enough to allow it to walk there without being seen, perhaps represented what best suited the bird's needs. To hide in there, for the present, waiting for night, which was now near; and afterwards, afterwards it would see what could be done. Because the land might not necessarily be entirely surrounded by water. How could it tell? The shoal might be connected, somehow, with the mainland. And having the mainland within walking distance would mean a further opportunity to escape, perhaps even salvation, or perhaps, if not definitive salvation, the almost certain guarantee of staying alive at least until tomorrow.

It went farther and farther away, in the meanwhile, painfully dragging its shattered wing after it; and he thought he could read in its narrow, obstinate little neck all this reasoning. But how mistaken it was, he suddenly said to himself, it fooled itself to such a degree (the strip of land was all right, it would get there; but with all the blood it was still shedding, the dog, soon unleashed to search for it, wouldn't have the slightest difficulty in flushing it), it was wrong to such a degree, obviously, poor stupid animal, that if he hadn't felt that shooting at it would seem, to him, shooting in a sense at himself, he would have fired at once. Then, at least, it would be all over.

GIORGIO BASSANI (1916–2000), Italy

Heron, F.O. Morris (1810–1893), Ireland/England

FROM IDOLS OF PERVERSITY

A QUICK GLANCE AT THE PAGES of such a magazine as
Jugend will convince anyone that the artists of the turn of the
century had read their Darwin and the writings of the bio-
sexists very diligently. Darwin had said that "the Asiatic
Antilope saiga appears to be the most inordinate polygamist in
the world" (*The Descent of Man*, 246), and, sure enough, *Jugend*
began featuring images of nude women riding at breakneck
speed on the backs of precisely such long-horned antelopes.
Other animals singled out by Darwin for their philandering
tendencies also attracted the attention of the ubiquitously
unclad lasses of what has been considered the German artistic renaissance. These young women consequently played
with wild boars, rode elephants as well as lions, and even
naughtily nudged seals. Artists also favored the conjunction of
women with extremely long-beaked fowl. One of these well-
endowed creatures paid his hopeful respects as a suitor to an
impressively unclad young lady in Richard Müller's "Lover's
Quest" . . . which was reproduced in *Jugend* in 1914. Max
Klinger, Gustave Moreau, and Félicien Rops, among many

Peacock Dance, A. Weisberger (1878–1915), Germany

131

others, also tapped this source of artistic inspiration. With the period's characteristic sense that more of a good thing is always likely to be better, the theme was finally pursued by Auguste Matisse, who, though in actual terms only a few years older, can be regarded, at least insofar as subject matter is concerned, as the far more famous Henri's spiritual painter-father. Auguste specialized in a form of decorative art considered "ideal" in its focus. This permitted him to produce such suggestive scenes of feminine life as his symphonic opus of 1905 entitled "In the Gold of the Evening" . . . which was composed of a swamp-sized congregation of delectable ladies and long-necked, long-beaked birds. The painting featured, in the foreground, among a cluster of nymphs, one young lady who understandably appeared to be concerned about her rounded exposure to the pointed attentions of an approaching cormorant. To suggest, as cultural historians have been wont to, that paintings such as these were naive, unconscious images of archetypal sexual symbols whose real meaning the psychoanalysts were in the process of uncovering at just this time represents a fundamental misunderstanding of the anything but unconscious prurience of the late nineteenth-century art world.

BRAM DIJKSTRA (1930–), Indonesia/United States

an Old Raven
5 April 1790

I MET WITH ONE of the most extraordinary phenomena that I ever saw, or heard of: —Mr Sellers has in his yard a large Newfoundland dog, and an old raven. They have fallen deeply in love with each other, and never desire to be apart. The bird has learned the bark of the dog, so that few can distinguish them. She is inconsolable when he goes out; and, if he stays out a day or two, she will get up all the bones and scraps she can, and hoard them up for him till he comes back.

JOHN WESLEY (1703–1791), England

The Arctic Raven, K. Pootoogook (1935–), Nunavut / Canada

FLOKI RELEASED A RAVEN

ARMED WITH STANDARD SAILING DIRECTIONS, and with a comprehensive knowledge of navigational methods, supplemented by a well-developed instinctive skill, Norse navigators stood every chance of making successful passages even over the dark waters of the Western Ocean. These men were not casual venturers upon the sea; they were highly professional and very competent seamen of a kind whose like has now all but vanished from the earth, under the influence of mechanical propulsion and the electronic navigator.

They were also brilliant improvisors. In the *Islendingabok* we read of the exploit of one Raven-Floki who wished to make a voyage to Iceland but who did not have sailing directions for the voyage. Floki set out to go there anyway, and as navigation aids he carried a number of ravens. Ravens, as Floki evidently knew, are land birds—and nonmigratory. They do not have to make passages across large expanses of open water, and seldom do so voluntarily. When a raven is freed from a ship it will promptly make for the nearest land it can see. From a height of 5000 feet—at which altitude the big black bird is still easily visible from sea level—a raven can probably see land ninety miles away, and high land a great deal farther off.

It is recorded that on the first day out of sight of the Faeroes, Floki released a raven, which circled a few times and then struck off on the vessel's back track, toward the Faeroes. On the second day another raven circled for a long time high in the pale sky, and finally returned to perch upon the vessel's mast. But on the next day, the raven climbed to a great height and then flew purposefully off toward the west. Following it with their eyes until it vanished, the Norsemen set their course by that of the bird and in due time raised the coast of Iceland.

Some people deride this account as being apocryphal. There is no reason to think that it is anything of the sort. On the contrary, the use of ravens by the sailor who later came to be called Raven-Floki was no more than what one might have expected from a seafaring people who were very closely attuned to the world in which they lived.

FARLEY MOWAT (1921–), Canada
from *Westviking*

Iceland or Gyr Falcon.

A Full Ten Thousand Falconers

Of the great khan's proceeding to the chase, with his gerfalcons and hawks—of his falconers—and of his tents.

When his majesty has resided the usual time in the metropolis, and leaves it in the month of March, he proceeds in a north-easterly direction, to within two days' journey of the ocean, attended by full ten thousand falconers, who carry with them a vast number of gerfalcons, peregrine falcons, and sakers, as well as many vultures, in order to pursue the game along the banks of the river. It must be understood that he does not keep all this body of men together in one place, but divides them into several parties of one or two hundred or more, who follow the sport in various directions, and the greater part of what they take is brought to his majesty. He has likewise with him ten thousand men of those who are termed taskaol, implying that their business is to be upon the watch, and, who, for this purpose, are detached in small parties of two or three to stations not far distant from each other, in such a manner as to encompass a considerable tract of country. Each of them is provided with a call and a hood, by

Iceland or Gyr Falcon, J.J. Audubon (1785–1851), France / United States

which they are enabled, when necessary, to call in and to secure the birds. Upon the command being given for flying the hawks, those who let them loose are not under the necessity of following them, because the others, whose duty it is, look out so attentively that the birds cannot direct their flight to any quarter where they are not secured, or promptly assisted if there should be occasion. Every bird belonging to his majesty, or to any of his nobles, has a small silver label fastened to its leg, on which is engraved the name of the owner and also the name of the keeper. In consequence of this precaution, as soon as the hawk is secured, it is immediately known to whom it belongs, and restored accordingly. If it happens that, although the name appears, the owner, not being personally known to the finder, cannot be ascertained in the first instance, the bird is, in that case, carried to an officer termed *bulangazi*, whose title imports that he is the "guardian of unclaimed property." If a horse, therefore, a sword, a bird, or any other article is found, and it does not appear to whom it belongs, the finder carries it directly to this officer, by whom it is received in charge and carefully preserved. If, on the other hand, a person finds any article that has been lost, and fails to carry it to the proper depositary, he is accounted a thief. Those by whom any property has been lost make their application to this officer, by whom it is restored to them. His situation is always in the most elevated part of the camp, and distinguished by a particular flag, in order that he may be the more readily found by such as have occasion to apply to him. The effect of this regulation is, that no articles are ultimately lost.

When his majesty makes his progress in this manner, towards the shores of the ocean, many interesting occurrences attend the sport, and it may truly be said that it is unrivalled by any other amusement in the world. On account of the narrowness of the passes in some parts of the country where the grand khan follows the chase, he is borne upon two elephants only, or sometimes a single one, being more convenient than a greater number; but under other circumstances he makes use of four, upon the backs of which is placed a pavilion of wood, handsomely carved, the inside being lined with cloth of gold, and the outside covered with the skins of lions, a mode of conveyance which is rendered necessary to him during his hunting excursions, in consequence of the gout, with which he is troubled. In the pavilion he always carries with him twelve of his best gerfalcons, with twelve officers, from amongst his favourites, to bear him company and amuse him. Those who are on horseback by his side give him notice of the approach of cranes or other birds, upon which he raises the curtain of the pavilion, and when he espies the game, gives direction for letting fly the gerfalcons, which seize the cranes and overpower them after a long struggle. The view of this sport, as he lies upon his couch, affords extreme satisfaction to his majesty, as well as to the officers who attend him, and to the horsemen by whom he is surrounded. After having thus enjoyed the amusement for some hours, he repairs to a place named Kakzarmodin, where are pitched the pavilions and tents of his sons, and also of the nobles, the life-guards, and the falconers; exceeding ten thousand in number, and making a handsome appearance.

MARCO POLO (1254–1324), Italy
from *The Travels of Marco Polo*

Phthisical Husband

The *Medical Record* TELLS of a woman in Ohio who utilized the high temperature of her phthisical husband for eight weeks before his death, by using him as an incubator for hens' eggs. She took 50 eggs, and wrapping each one in cotton batting, laid them alongside the body of her husband in the bed, he being unable to resist or move a limb. After three weeks she was rewarded with forty-six lively young chickens.

SCIENTIFIC AMERICAN

HURT HAWKS

I

The broken pillar of the wing jags from the clotted
        shoulder,
The wing trails like a banner in defeat,
No more to use the sky forever but live with famine
And pain a few days: cat nor coyote
Will shorten the week of waiting for death, there is
        game without talons.
He stands under the oak bush and waits
The lame feet of salvation; at night he remembers
        freedom
And flies in a dream, the dawns ruin it.
He is strong and pain is worse to the strong, incapacity
        is worse.

Bird Preparing to Fly, O. Mikkigak (1936–), Nunavut/Canada

The curs of the day come and torment him
At distance, no one but death the redeemer will humble
    that head,
The intrepid readiness, the terrible eyes.
The wild God of the world is sometimes merciful to those
That ask mercy, not often to the arrogant.
You do not know him, you communal people, or you
    have forgotten him;
Intemperate and savage, the hawk remembers him;
Beautiful and wild, the hawks, and men that are dying,
    remember him.

II

I'd sooner, except the penalties, kill a man than a hawk;
    but the great redtail
Had nothing left but unable misery
From the bone too shattered for mending, the wing
    that trailed under his talons when he moved.
We had fed him six weeks, I gave him freedom,
He wandered over the foreland hill and returned in the
    evening, asking for death,
Not like a beggar, still eyed with the old
Implacable arrogance. I gave him the lead gift in the
    twilight. What fell was relaxed,
Owl-downy, soft feminine feathers; but what
Soared: the fierce rush: the night-herons by the flooded
    river cried fear at its rising
Before it was quite unsheathed from reality.

ROBINSON JEFFERS (1885–1962), United States

BIRDS

CAME THE YELLOW DAYS of winter, filled with boredom. The rust-coloured earth was covered with a threadbare, meagre tablecloth of snow full of holes. There was not enough of it for some of the roofs and so they stood there, black and brown, shingle and thatch, arks containing the sooty expanses of attics—coal-black cathedrals, bristling with ribs of rafters, beams and spars—the dark lungs of winter winds. Each dawn revealed new chimney stacks and chimney pots which had emerged during the hours of darkness, blown up by the night winds: the black pipes of a Devil's organ. The chimney-sweeps could not get rid of the crows which in the evening covered the branches of the trees around the church with living black leaves, then took off, fluttering, and came back, each clinging to its own place on its own branch, only to fly away at dawn in large flocks, like gusts of soot, flakes of dirt, undulating and fantastic, blackening with their insistent crowing the musty-yellow streaks of light. The days hardened with cold and boredom like last year's loaves of bread. One began to cut them with blunt knives without appetite, with a lazy indifference.

Father had stopped going out. He banked up the stoves,

studied the ever elusive essence of fire, experienced the salty, metallic taste and the smoky smell of wintry flames, the cool caresses of salamanders that licked the shiny soot in the throat of the chimney. He applied himself lovingly at that time to all manner of small repairs in the upper regions of the rooms. At all hours of the day one could see him crouched on top of a ladder, working at something under the ceiling, at the cornices over the tall windows, at the counter-weights and chains of the hanging lamps. Following the custom of house painters, he used a pair of steps as enormous stilts and he felt perfectly happy in that bird's eye perspective close to the sky, leaves and birds painted on the ceiling. He grew more and more remote from practical affairs. When my mother, worried and unhappy about his condition, tried to draw him into a conversation about business, about the payments due at the end of the month, he listened to her absent-mindedly, anxiety showing in his abstracted look. Sometimes he stopped her with a warning gesture of the hand in order to run to a corner of the room, put his ear to a crack in the floor and, by lifting the index finger of both hands, emphasise the gravity of the investigation, and begin to listen intently. At that time we did not yet understand the sad origin of these eccentricities, the deplorable complex which had been maturing in him.

Mother had no influence over him, but he gave a lot of respectful attention to Adela. The cleaning of his room was to him a great and important ceremony, of which he always arranged to be a witness, watching all Adela's movements with a mixture of apprehension and pleasurable excitement. He ascribed to all her functions a deeper, symbolic meaning.

Aboriginal rock art figures from the Cobar region, classed as emus (c.2,000BC), Australia

When, with young firm gestures, the girl pushed a long-handled broom along the floor, father could hardly bear it. Tears would stream from his eyes, silent laughter transformed his face and his body was shaken by spasms of delight. He was ticklish to the point of madness. It was enough for Adela to waggle her fingers at him to imitate tickling, for him to rush through all the rooms in a wild panic, banging the doors after him, to fall at last flat on the bed in the furthest room and wriggle in convulsions of laughter, imagining the tickling which he found irresistible. Because of this, Adela's power over father was almost limitless.

At that time we noticed for the first time father's passionate interest in animals. To begin with, it was the passion of the huntsman and the artist rolled into one. It was almost perhaps a deeper, biological sympathy of one creature for kindred, yet different forms of life, a kind of experimenting in the unexplored regions of existence. Only at a later stage did matters take that uncanny, complicated, essentially sinful and unnatural turn, which it is better not to bring into the light of day.

But it all began with the hatching out of birds' eggs.

With a great outlay of effort and money, father imported from Hamburg, or Holland, or from zoological stations in Africa, birds' eggs on which he set enormous broody hens from Belgium. It was a process which fascinated me as well—this hatching out of the chicks, which were real anomalies of shape and colour. It was difficult to anticipate in these monsters with enormous, fantastic beaks which they opened wide immediately after birth, hissing greedily to show the backs of their throats, in these lizards with frail, naked bodies of hunchbacks, the future peacocks, pheasants, grouse or condors. Placed in cotton-wool, in baskets, this dragon brood lifted blind, wall-eyed heads on thin necks, croaking voicelessly from their dumb throats. My father would walk along the shelves, dressed in a green baize apron like a gardener in a hothouse of cacti, and conjure up from nothingness these blind bubbles, pulsating with life, these impotent bellies receiving the outside world only in the form of food, these growths on the surface of life, climbing blindfold towards the light. A few weeks' later when these blind buds of matter burst open, the rooms were filled with the bright chatter and scintillating chirruping of its new inhabitants. The birds perched on the curtain pelmets, on the tops of wardrobes; they nestled in the tangle of tin branches and the metal scrolls of the hanging lamps.

While father pored over his large ornithological textbooks and studied their coloured plates, these feathery phantasms seemed to rise from the pages and fill the rooms with colours, with splashes of crimson, strips of sapphire, verdigris and silver. At feeding time they formed a motley, undulating bed on the floor, a living carpet which at the intrusion of a stranger would fall apart, scatter into fragments, flutter in the air, and finally settle high under the ceilings. I remember in particular a certain condor, an enormous bird with a featherless neck, its face wrinkled and knobbly. It was an emaciated ascetic, a Buddhist lama, full of imperturbable dignity in its behaviour, guided by the rigid ceremonial of its great species. When it sat facing my father, motionless in the monumental position of ageless Egyptian idols, its eye covered with a whitish cataract which it pulled down sideways over its pupil to shut itself up completely in the contemplation of its dignified solitude—it seemed, with its stony profile, like an older brother of my father's. Its body and muscles seemed to be made of the same material, it had the same hard, wrinkled skin, the same desiccated bony face, the same horny deep eye sockets. Even the hands, strong in the joints, my father's long thick hands with their rounded nails, had their counterpart in the condor's claws. I could not resist the impression, when looking at the sleeping condor, that I was in the presence of a mummy—a dried out, shrunken mummy of my father. I believe that even my mother noticed this strange resemblance although we never discussed the subject. It is significant that the condor used my father's chamberpot.

Not content with the hatching out of more and more new specimens, my father arranged the marriages of birds in the attic, he sent out matchmakers, he tied up eager attractive brides in the holes and crannies under the roof, and soon the roof of our house, an enormous double-ridged shingle roof, became a real birds' hostel, a Noah's ark to which all kinds of feathery creatures flew from far afield. Long after the liquidation of the birds' paradise, this tradition persisted in the avian world and during the period of spring migration our roof was besieged by whole flocks of cranes, pelicans, peacocks and sundry other birds. However, after a short period of splendour, the whole undertaking took a sorry turn.

It soon became necessary to move my father to two rooms at the top of the house which had served as box rooms. We could hear from there, at dawn, the mixed clangour of birds' voices. The wooden walls of the attic rooms, helped by the resonance of the empty space under the gables, sounded with the roar, the flutterings, the crowing, the gurgling, the mating cries. For a few weeks father was lost to view. He only rarely came down to the flat and, when he did, we noticed that he seemed to have shrunk, to have become smaller and thinner. Occasionally forgetting himself, he would rise from his chair at table, wave his arms as if they were wings, and emit a long-drawn-out bird's call while his eyes misted over. Then, rather embarrassed, he would join us in laughing it off and try to turn the whole incident into a joke.

One day, during spring cleaning, Adela suddenly appeared in father's birds' kingdom. Stopping in the doorway, she wrung her hands at the foetid smell that filled the room, the heaps of droppings covering the floor, the tables and the chairs. Without hesitation, she flung open a window and, with the help of a long broom, she prodded the whole mass of birds into life. A fiendish cloud of feathers and wings arose screaming and Adela, like a furious Maenad protected by the whirlwind of her thyrsus, danced the dance of destruction. My father, waving his arms in panic, tried to lift himself into the air with his feathered flock. Slowly the winged cloud thinned until at last Adela remained on the battlefield, exhausted and out of breath, along with my father who now, adopting a worried hang dog expression, was ready to accept complete defeat.

A moment later, my father came downstairs—a broken man, an exiled king who had lost his throne and his kingdom.

BRUNO SCHULZ (1892–1942), Poland

T'is a beautiful belief
That ever round our head
Are hov'ring on angel's wings
The Spirits of the dead.

ANON

Quoth the Raven, Nevermore.

EDGAR ALLAN POE

v ~

A BIRD IN THE HOUSE

Sinister auspices

Barn Owl, H.C. Richter (1821–1902), Germany

IF YOU LOOK UP BIRDS in an encyclopedia of superstitions, you'll find they feature prominently. With notable exceptions—the wren, for example, and the robin—they speak of misfortune. If the owl calls your name, you're doomed; you're similarly doomed, among the Irish, if you have peacock feathers in your house. Pigeons settling on the roof are bad luck, wheeling gulls are the souls of drowned sailors, and when Europeans heard the first cuckoo of Spring, the number of notes it sang told the listener how many years remained until his death.

A fascination with predictions and premonitions retains a spectral existence in our lives. When we lived in the country we had friends whose house had been in the family since the 1840s. The wife, whom I'll call Betty, was known for her "raven knowledge." Occasionally she'd smell blood in her stairwell and predict a fatality, or at least some terrible injury. One of Betty's sayings was that a bird in the house meant a death in the house.

Wild birds in the house, or even beating against the window, foretell death because they suggest the idea of frantic wandering souls. Nor is it surprising that birds are associated with prophecy. Like angels, they are of the air rather than the earth, of the spirit rather than the body. They can move between worlds, and are therefore messengers from the gods. Who better to know what's really going on—or about to go on?

Birds can also inform the observant in simpler ways:

> If the Emperor Napoleon, when on the road to Moscow with his army in 1811, had condescended to observe the flights of storks and cranes passing over his fated battalions, subsequent events in the politics of Europe might have been very different. These storks and cranes knew of the coming on of a great and terrible winter; the birds hastened towards the south, Napoleon and his army towards the north.[1]

On one level, "augury" is merely a talent for reading the signs. But reading an early migration as the sign of a harsh winter, and reading a frantic bird battering itself against the window as a harbinger of death, speak to radically different sets of assumptions. One has to do with natural history, the other with superstition and religious beliefs.

Yet both worlds come together when we hear of the diminishing of birds in our world—the extinction of whole species, the collapsing numbers of remaining ones. On one level, the signs tell us that the dying birds are the canaries in the coal mine: there's poison in the air, and we'll be next. On the other level, the killing of birds is the killing of the spirit.

In the New Testament, Christ claims that not a single sparrow falls without God noticing it. We ourselves have not been nearly so attentive. Will the Raven's 'Nevermore' apply, soon, not to the lost Lenore, but to all the birds we have somehow managed to extinguish forever?

G.G.

1. Frank Buckland, in George C. Bompas's *Life of Frank Buckland*, 1885

BLACKBIRD

A blackbird sat on a TV antenna
and sang a gentle, jazzy tune.
Whom have you lost, I asked, what do you mourn?
I'm taking leave of those who've gone, the blackbird said,
I'm parting with the day (its eyes and lashes),
I mourn a girl who lived in Thrace,
you wouldn't know her.
I'm sorry for the willow, killed by frost.
I weep, since all things pass and alter
and return, but always in a different form.
My narrow throat can barely hold
the grief, despair, delight, and pride
occasioned by such sweeping transformations.
A funeral cortege passes up ahead,
the same each evening, there, on the horizon's thread.
Everyone's there. I see them all and bid farewell.
I see the swords, hats, kerchiefs, and bare feet,
guns, blood, and ink. They walk slowly
and vanish in the river mist, on the right bank.
I say goodbye to them and you and the light,
and then I greet the night, since I serve her—
and black silks, black powers.

ADAM ZAGAJEWSKI (1945–), Poland

CHORUS FROM AGAMEMNON

Although I'm old—perhaps because of it—
I am the man to sing you the true story,
With the clear power
The years and gods have given.

Over ten years ago our brother kings set sail,
Their ships bristling with spears,
Carrying vengeance north—
When two great birds, the birds of Zeus,
Eagles, one black, one marked with white,
Flew overhead, to the right—
The spear-hand side! Omen of victory!

But then they stooped, and chased
A hare pregnant with babies,
And tore her open.
The royal black, the royal white-marked eagle
Devoured the living unborn young
Within their mother.

My song is pitiful. May good follow all evil.

Then Calchas, our great seer, saw deep
Into the meaning hidden in this act:
The two birds were two kings,
Our kings and leaders, Menelaus
And Agamemnon. Brothers, both sons
Of the House of Atreus.
He prophesied: "Victory—true.

But victory at a price.
Troy can be yours—you'll rip it open,
You'll kill its young, you'll feast
In triumph over their murdered flesh.
Priam is doomed—his city's doomed
To die in violence, no matter
How many flocks and herd-beasts
His priests slaughter,
Praying for safety.
But beware, all you who think
You're set to humble Troy—
For silver Artemis, the virgin
Protectress of pregnant mothers,
And shield of their innocent young—
She too has seen this omen. She too
Knows what it means. She hates
The foul deed done by the twin birds
Of Father Zeus. The violation
Of the mother-shrine
That shadows forth the greater violation
Our kings intend.

My song is pitiful. May good follow all evil.

Then Calchas, still in his
Prophetic trance, invoked the goddess:
Radiant Artemis, goddess of wild animals,
Tender to all their young,
Hold back your anger!
Restrain the evil in this sign,
Unloose good fortune!

Apollo, god of healing,
Intervene with your sister—
Let her not pen our fleet
With an ill wind in some island bay,
Keeping us there until our brother kings
Are forced to pay
With the blood of another sacrifice—
A beautiful young creature,
Adored and cherished,
Her death unsanctified,
Leaving a bitter poison in the mind, slayer
Of family trust, bringer of dark terror
And angry hatred
To the house that sent it forth.
A child's murder will return
Upon you, vengeance
In the blood footprints.

This is what Calchas said. This is how
He uncoded the meaning of the two birds:
This is the warning he gave, of good fortune
For the kings' house entwined with ill.

My song is pitiful; may good follow all evil.

AESCHYLUS (525–456BC), Greece

OVERLEAF: Illustration from *Le Pèlerin*, no. 2329 (November 1921).
E. Damblans (b. 1865), France

157

En Colombie britannique, un aigle essaye d'enlever une fillette de

: on a pu délivrer l'enfant et tuer l'oiseau de proie. (Dessin de DAMBLANS)

Le Hibou Blanc

IT WAS A STILL DAY late in September. . . . Madame Blais sat on an upturned box on the narrow gallery that ran the length of the summer kitchen. She was plaiting long strings of red onions to hang in the attic for the winter. . . .

She didn't often get such a good day for work. Her mind was turning in a placid, peaceful circle, *"Que tous s'adone bien aujourd-hui."*

Suddenly the peace was broken. Puppay had begun to bark furiously; then the barking changed to joyful yapping. . . .

Me'mère had heard the noise too and had come to the door. "What is it?" she asked, *"Un Jerusalem?"* "No," answered Madame, "it's the men coming home, and it's not yet four. Something must have happened."

Owl with a Human Face, S. Ashoona (1928–1970), Nunavut/Canada

She watched the men anxiously as they crossed the field. She noticed that Felix wasn't with them. As they came up to the house she called out, "What has happened?"

No one answered her; the men tramped on in silence. When they got to the house, her husband sat down on the step of the gallery and began taking off his *bottes-sauvages*. The other two and the children stood watching him.

"Where is Felix?" asked Madame.

"He wouldn't come with us."

"Why did you leave so early?"

Again there was silence; then her husband said, "We saw the Hibou Blanc."

"You saw him?"

"Yes," answered her husband, "that's why we came home."

"Why didn't Felix come with you?"

"He said it was all nonsense. Old men's stories."

"You should have made him come with you," said Me'Mère. "You can't remember the last time the Hibou Blanc came. But I can. It was just two years after I was married. Bonté Lemay was like Felix, he didn't believe. He stayed on ploughing when the others left. The horse got scared and ran away. Bonté's arm was caught in the reins and he was dragged after the plough. His head struck a stone and he was dead when they found him. His poor mother. How she cried. One doesn't make fun of the Hibou Blanc."

. . . "Do you think Felix will have the sense to come home?" asked Madame.

Joseph shook his head and spat skilfully into the brown earthenware spittoon.

"No fear," he answered. "He says in the States they have

162

more sense than to believe all those old stories."

"If Felix stays on in the woods, harm will certainly come to him," said Me'mère, "I tell you the Hibou Blanc always brings disaster."

"Why don't you go and speak to the Curé?" said Madame Blais.

"He's away at Rimouski for a retreat," answered Exdras. . . .

"Well, it's time to get the cows," said Monsieur Blais. "Go along and get them, Joseph."

The autumn evenings close in quickly in the north. By the time the cows were milked and supper finished, the clear cold green of evening had swept up over the sky; the stars were out, and the little silver crescent of the moon had risen over the maple wood. Joseph was sitting out on the step of the little gallery, his eyes fastened on the break in the maple wood that marked the road leading to the sugar cabin. Every now and then his father went out and joined him. They were both watching for Felix.

As the kitchen clock began to strike eight Madame put down her work. "It's time for the Rosary," she said. "Tell Joseph to come in." Her husband opened the door and called to Joseph. He came in, followed by Puppay.

The family pulled their chairs up round the stove, for the evenings were beginning to be chilly, and it was cold away from the stove.

Me'Mère began the Rosary: *"Je crois en Dieu, le Père tout-puissant. . . ."* The quiet murmur of their voices filled the kitchen.

When the Rosary was said Madame sent the children off to bed. Then she went to the salon and got a *cierge bénit,* lit it, and put it in the kitchen window. "May God have pity on him," she said. Then she picked up p'tit Charles and went off to bed with her husband, while Me'mère went to her little room next to the salon.

It was bright and cold the next day, and the ground was covered with white hoar-frost.

Joseph was the first to speak of Felix. "He may have gone and slept with one of the neighbours," he said.

"If he did he'd be back by now," answered his father.

They were still eating their breakfast when Exdras Boulay came into the kitchen.

"Felix hasn't come back?" he asked.

Before anyone could answer, the door opened and two other neighbours came in. The news of Felix and the Hibou Blanc had already spread along the road. Soon there were eight men and boys in the kitchen and half a dozen excited children.

The men sat round in the kitchen smoking. Old Alphonse Ouellet did most of the talking. He was always the leader in the parish.

"We'll have to go and find him," he said.

"It's too bad the Curé isn't here to come with us. Well, we might as well start off now. Bring your rosary with you," he told Monsieur Blais.

Madame Blais and Me'Mère and a group of the children stood on the kitchen gallery watching the men as they tramped off along the rough track to the maple wood.

"May God have them in His care," said Madame.

"And may He have pity on Felix," added Me'Mère, and she crossed herself.

In the maple wood the ground was still covered with frost. Every little hummock of fallen leaves was white with it, and the puddles along the track were frozen solid. The men walked in silence. A secret fear gripped each one of them that they might suddenly see the Hibou Blanc perched on some old stump, or one of the snow-covered hummocks. A few hundred yards from the sugar cabin they found Felix. He was lying on his back. His red shirt looked at first like a patch of red maple leaves lying in the hoar-frost. A great birch had fallen across his chest, pinning him to the ground. One of his hands was grasping a curl of the bark—his last mad effort to try and free himself.

The men stood round staring down at him, the immense silence of the woods surrounding them. Then from far away in the distance came a thin whinnying note; the shrill triumphant cry of *Le Hibou Blanc*.

Traditional Quebecois legend
in Boswell, *Legends of Quebec*

FROM TE MANU TUKUTUKU: THE MAORI KITE

THE MAORI WERE ABLE TO USE the flight of a kite as a means of divination. Should a kite swoop to earth and be destroyed, the event would be seen as a warning from the gods. Prior to the famous battle of Orakau Pa in 1864, Rewi Maniapoto, war chief of the Ngati Maniapoto tribe and defender of its stronghold received an omen:

> He had dreamed, he told his people, that he was standing outside the church in Orakau and flying a kite, one of the large bird-shaped kites made of raupo and adorned with feathers. At first it soared strongly upwards to the clouds, then it broke loose and came to the ground in pieces. The shattering of the kite he interpreted as a portent of the utter defeat of the Maoris.

The siege and capture of the pa by British troops marked the end of the Waikato wars and the loss, by government confiscation, of massive tracts of Maori land.

BOB MAYSMOR (contemporary), New Zealand

ABOVE: *Birdman Kite,* Maori (19th century)
OPPOSITE: *Birdman Kite* (detail), Maori (1843)

BIRD-CAGE

I am a bird-cage

A cage of bones
With a bird in it

That bird in the bony cage
is death, building his nest

When nothing goes on
We can hear his wings clashing

After a good deal of laughter
If we stop suddenly
We can hear him cooing
Deep down
Like a small bell

Death is a captive bird
Kept in my cage of bones

Wouldn't he like to fly away
Is it you who keep him
Is it I
What is it

He will not leave until
He has eaten all of me
My heart
The source of blood
And the life inside

He will have my soul in his beak

HECTOR SAINT-DENYS-GARNEAU (1912–1943), Canada

Buntings, A.F. Lydon (1836–1917), England

Soo-Koo'-Me
the Great Horned Owl

The Middle Mewuk of Tuolumne River foothills say:

When Soo-koo'-me the Great Horned Owl hoots, it means someone is dying. He is himself the Ghosts of dead people.

(I was once asked by a Northern Mewuk if I had ever seen the broad belt of bony plates which surround the eyeball of the Great Horned Owl. On replying that I had, I was assured that these closely imbricating plates are the "finger nails all jammed tight together of the ghosts caught by the owl.")

Traditional Miwok tale, United States
in Merriam, *The Dawn of the World*

Great Horned Owl, T.M. Shortt (1911–1986), Canada

Hagen and the Owls at Glencoe

There's a touch of the witch,
A shaft of God between the clouds
A death in the house, and life
Is a cobweb of glass.

The cat's buried at the river,
His death weighs like water in a sack
The owls that cry in the night-time
dropped us a mouse with no back.

Such things by the door in the morning!
Things to keep you knowing
That God is in the potting shed,
Puts your eye to a crack between the slats.

KATHLEEN JAMIE (1962–), Scotland

THE WOMAN WHO WAS A BIRD

THERE WAS THIS MAN who had a son and married a second time, but what he didn't know was that his new wife was really a garlin, or egret. Now every time she cooked him his peas and rice and meat, she would tell him she didn't want any because she wasn't feeling well. Then when her husband went out to work she turned back into a garlin and went out to the pond and caught crabs and ate her belly full, and made haste to come back home and return into a person before her husband came back. Each time, just as her husband left, she would go inside the bedroom and shed her clothes and begin to sing:

> *Kitty Katty kee wang wah,*
> *Kitty Katty wang wah wah,*
> *Kitty Katty kee wang wah,*
> *Kitty Katty wang wah.*
> *Kee* bottom, *kee* bottom, *kee pyang,*
> *Kitty Katty kee wang wah, kee pyang.*

Then two wings would come out. She would sing again:

> *Kitty Katty kee wang wah,*
> *Kitty Katty wang wah wah,*
> *Kitty Katty kee wang wah,*
> *Kitty Katty wang wah.*
> *Kee* bottom, *kee* bottom, *kee pyang,*
> *Kitty Katty kee wang wah, kee pyang.*

Golden-Collared Macaw, M.O. Des Murs (b. 1804), France

Her feathers would come out on her. She would sing again:

Kitty Katty kee wang wah,
Kitty Katty wang wah wah,
Kitty Katty kee wang wah,
Kitty Katty wang wah.
Kee bottom, kee bottom, kee pyang,
Kitty Katty kee wang wah, kee pyang.

A bill would come out. And then she would fly out the window and go to the pond and catch crabs.

Now the man's son suspected his stepmother wasn't a person, so he kept watch on her. One day he stayed home after his father had gone, and as he was watching, he heard her sing her song and saw her turn into a garlin again.

And when his father came back that night, the little boy said, "Poppa, this wife that you have isn't really a person; she's a garlin." "What is that you say, boy? This couldn't be." "Yes, Poppa, she is a garlin. If you don't believe me, keep watch on her like I did this morning when you leave for work." And he described what had happened, and sang the song for his father.

The next day the garlin-wife cooked her husband's breakfast. He ate some, and so did the little boy, but she wouldn't eat anything. Her husband asked her why, and she said, "I'm feeling sick. No, no, husband, I just can't eat anything this morning." Her husband went and got his gun, loaded it up and he began to sing:

Kitty Katty kee wang wah,
Kitty Katty wang wah wah,
Kitty Katty kee wang wah,
Kitty Katty wang wah.
Kee bottom, *kee* bottom, *kee pyang,*
Kitty Katty kee wang wah, kee pyang.

Now as he sang that song she burst out crying, "Don't, husband, don't sing that. Every time you sing that song, it makes me remember my dead mother." She knew if he kept going, she would turn into a bird right in front of him, but he sang it anyhow. First time, though, her legs came out, and the second time it was her wings:

Kitty Katty kee wang wah,
Kitty Katty wang wah wah,
Kitty Katty kee wang wah,
Kitty Katty wang wah.
Kee bottom, *kee* bottom, *kee pyang,*
Kitty Katty kee wang wah, kee pyang.

He sang it until her feet came out, her feathers, and then her bill. He took his gun then, and killed her.

Traditional Bahamian folktale
in Abrahams, *Afro-American Folktales*

PROUD MASIE

Proud Masie is in the wood
   Walking so early;
Sweet Robin sits on the bush,
   Singing so rarely.

"Tell me thou bonny bird,
   When shall I marry me?"—
"When six braw gentlemen
   Kirkward shall carry ye."

"Who makes the bridal bed,
   Birdie, say truly?"—
"The gray-headed sexton
   That delves the grave duly.

"The glow-worm o'er grave and stone
   Shall light thee steady,
The owl from the steeple sing,
   Welcome, proud lady."

SIR WALTER SCOTT (1771–1832), Scotland

European Robin, K. Svolinsky (1896–1986), Czech

Last Comes the Raven

The current was a network of light transparent ripples with the water flowing in the middle. Every now and again silver wings seemed to flutter on the surface, a trout's back glittering before it zigzagged down.

"It's full of trout," said one of the men.

"If we throw a grenade in, they'll all come to the surface with their bellies in the air," said the other; he took a grenade from his belt and began to unscrew the cap.

Then a boy who was watching stepped forward, a mountaineer with an apple face. "Give it to me," he said and took the rifle from one of the men. "What does he want?" said the man and tried to take the rifle away. But the boy was aiming the gun at the water as if looking for a target. "If you fire into the water you'll frighten the fish, that's all," the man tried to say, but he didn't even finish. A trout had surfaced with a flash, and the boy had fired a shot at it as if expecting it at that very spot. And the trout was now floating with its white belly in the air. "O-o-oh!" said the men. The boy reloaded the gun and swung it around; the air was bright and tight; the pine needles on the other bank and the ripples on the current showed up clearly. Something darted, to the surface; another trout. He fired; it was floating, dead. The men looked at the trout and then at him. "He's a good shot, this kid," they said.

The boy swung the muzzle of the gun around again. It was strange, thinking it over, to be so surrounded by air, separated from other things by yards of air. When he aimed the gun, on the other hand, the air was a straight invisible line drawn tight from the mouth of the rifle to the target, to the hawk flying up there in the sky with wings that did not seem to move. When he pressed the trigger, the air was still as empty and transparent as before, but up there, at the other end of the line, the hawk was folding its wings and dropping like a stone. From the open bolt floated the good smell of gunpowder.

They gave him some more cartridges when he asked for them. Lots of men were looking on now from the bank behind him. Why, he thought, could he see the pine cones at the tops of the trees on the other bank and not touch them? Why was there this empty distance between things and himself? Why were the pine cones—which seemed part of him, inside his eyes—so far away instead? Surely it was an illusion when he aimed the gun into the empty distance and touched the trigger and at the same second a pine cone dropped in smithereens? The sense of emptiness felt like a caress—emptiness inside the rifle barrel continuing through the air and filling out when he shot; the pine cone up there, a squirrel, a white stone, a butterfly. "He never misses once, this kid," said the men, and none of them felt like laughing.

"You come with us," said the commander. "If you give me a rifle," replied the boy. "Well, of course." So he went.

He left with two cheeses and a haversack full of apples. The village was a blotch of slate, straw, and cow dung at the bottom of the valley. It was fine to leave, because there were new things to be seen at every turn, trees with cones, birds flying from branches, lichen on stones, all at those false distances, the distances that could be filled by a shot swallowing the air in between. He must not fire, though, they told him: these parts had to be passed in silence, and the cartridges were needed for the war. But at a certain point a hare, frightened by their steps, ran across the path amid waves and shouts from the men. Just as it was vanishing into the thickets, a bullet from the boy stopped it. "Good shot," even the commander said, "but we're not out hunting here. You mustn't fire again even if you see a pheasant." Not an hour passed before more shots rang out from the file of men. "That boy again!" cried the commander furiously and went up to him. The boy was laughing all over his pink-and-white apple face. "Partridges," he said, showing them. "They rose from a thicket." "Partridges or grasshoppers, I told you. Give me that rifle. And if you make me angry again, you go back home." The boy grumbled a bit; it wasn't much fun walking along unarmed; but if he stayed with them there was always a chance of getting the rifle back.

That night they slept in a shepherd's hut. The boy woke up as the first light was showing in the sky, while the others were asleep. He took their best rifle, filled his haversack with cartridges, and took off. The early-morning air was mild and bright. Not far from the hut was a mulberry tree. It was the hour when the jays arrived. There was one; he fired, ran to fetch it, and put it in his haversack. Without moving from the spot he tried another target; a squirrel! Terrified by the shot, it was running to hide at the top of a chestnut tree. Now it was dead, a big squirrel with a gray tail, which shed tufts of hair when touched. From under the chestnut tree he saw a toadstool, red with white spots, poisonous, in a meadow lower down. He pulverized it with a shot, then went to see if he had really hit it. It was a lovely game going like this from one target to another; perhaps he could go around the world doing it. He saw a big snail on a stone and aimed at its shell; when he got to the place he found only the splintered stone and a little iridescent slime.

So he gradually got farther and farther away from the hut, down among unknown fields. From the stone he saw a lizard on a wall, from the wall a puddle and a frog, from the puddle a signpost on the road with a zigzag on it and below it . . . below it were men in uniform coming up with arms at the ready. When they saw that boy with a rifle smiling all over his pink-and-white apple face, they shouted and aimed their guns at him. But the boy had already picked out some gilt buttons on the chest of one of them and fired at a button. He heard the men's shouts and the bullets whistling singly or in bursts over his head; but he was now lying stretched on the ground behind a heap of stones at the roadside, under cover. It was a long heap, and he could move about, peep over at some unexpected point, see the gleam on the barrels of the soldiers' weapons, the gray and glittering parts of their uniforms, shoot at a stripe, a badge. Then he'd drop back to the ground and slide quickly over to another side to fire. After a bit he heard bursts from behind him firing over his head and hitting the soldiers; these were his comrades coming to reinforce him with machine guns. "If that boy hadn't woken us with his shots . . ." they were saying.

Covered by his comrades' fire, the boy could take better aim. Suddenly a bullet grazed one of his cheeks. He turned; a soldier had reached the road above him. He flung himself into a hole under cover, but had fired meanwhile and hit not the soldier but the rifle, by the bolt. He heard the soldier trying to reload, then fling the gun on the ground. The boy looked out then and fired at the soldier, who'd taken to his heels; the bullet tore off a shoulder strap.

He followed. Every now and again the soldier vanished in the wood, then reappeared. The boy nipped off the top of his helmet, then a strap on his belt. Meanwhile they had reached a remote valley where the sound of battle didn't reach. Suddenly the soldier found there were no more woods in front of him, only a glade, with thick bushy slopes. The boy was just coming out of the wood now; in the middle of the glade was a big rock; the soldier just had time to crouch down behind it, with his head between his knees. There for the moment he felt safe; he had some hand grenades with him and the boy could get no nearer, but could only keep the rock covered in case the soldier tried to escape. If only, thought the soldier, he could make a run for the bushes and slide down the thickly covered slope. But that bare space had to be crossed— how long would the boy stay there? And would he never lower that gun?

The soldier decided to make a test; he put his helmet on the point of his bayonet and hoisted it slightly above the rock. A shot rang out and the helmet rolled to the ground, pierced through.

The soldier did not lose heart; it was obviously easy to aim at the edges of the rock, but if he moved quickly it should be impossible to hit him. At that moment a bird winged quickly across the sky, a pigeon perhaps. One shot and it fell. The soldier dried the sweat on his neck. Another bird passed, a thrush; that fell, too. The soldier swallowed saliva. This must be a place of passage; birds went on flying overhead, all of them different, and the boy went on shooting and bringing them down. An idea came to the soldier: "If he is watching the birds he won't be watching me so much. The second he fires I'll run for it." But perhaps it would be better to make a test first. He took up the helmet again and put it back on the point of his bayonet, ready. Two birds passed together, snipe. The soldier was sorry to waste such a good opportunity for the test, but he did not dare risk it yet. The boy fired at one of the snipe, then the soldier pushed up the helmet, heard the shot and saw the helmet whirl in the air.

Now the soldier felt a taste of lead in his mouth; he scarcely noticed the other bird falling at a new shot. He must not hurry things, anyway; he was safe behind that rock, with his grenades. And why not try and get him with a grenade, while staying under cover? He stretched back on the ground, drew his arm out behind him, taking care not to show himself, gathered up all his strength and threw the grenade. A good effort; it would have gone a long way; but in the middle of its flight a shot exploded it in mid-air. The soldier flung himself on the ground to avoid the shrapnel.

When he raised his head the raven had come. It was wheeling slowly around in the sky above him. Was it a raven? he wondered. Now the boy would be certain to shoot it down. But the shot seemed to be a long time in coming. Perhaps the raven was flying too high? And yet he had hit other birds flying higher and faster. Finally there was a shot; now the raven would fall, but no, it went on flying around in slow impassive turns. A pine cone fell though, from a tree nearby. Was he beginning to shoot at pine cones now? One by one other pine cones were hit and fell with little thuds. At every shot the soldier looked at the raven; was he falling? No, the black bird was making lower and lower turns above him. Surely it was impossible the boy hadn't seen it? Perhaps the raven did not exist? Perhaps it was a hallucination of his? Perhaps when one is about to die one sees every kind of bird pass; when one sees the raven it means one's time has come. He must warn the boy. who was still going on firing at the pine cones. So the soldier got to his feet and pointed at the black bird. "There's a raven!" he shouted in his own language. The bullet hit him in the middle of an eagle with spread wings embroidered on his tunic.

Slowly the raven came circling down.

ITALO CALVINO (1923–1985), Cuba/Italy

If only I were hiding under the cliffs,
in secret among the rocks,
and that Zeus might transform me into a flying bird.

EURIPIDES

VI ~

REMEMBERING
IS NOT SEEING

Correspondences and transformations

The Swan Poet Dances with His Maidens, Codex Manesse (1315)

Once Siegfried has killed the Dragon in Wagner's well-known opera, he understands the language of birds. Not only that, what the bird tells him gives him a critical advantage over his enemies, and leads him to his true love, Brunnhilde. What does Wagner's bird represent? Fate, luck, a guiding spirit, the voice of nature, or Siegfried's own inner sight in visible form? In opera, as in dreams, birds can be symbols of the dreamer's personality.

We might speculate that birdwatchers on the prowl are unconsciously hoping to experience something of their better selves. Perhaps our engagement with the birds is an instinctive quest. If so we should remember that the results of quests can be unpredictable: we never know what we will discover. We might even find there is something greedy in us, a wish to control birds by naming them. On the other hand, we might uncover something wonderful within ourselves.

Thirty-five years ago, at the beginning of my birdwatching days, I found myself impatient to see a Pileated Woodpecker. Dashing and crow-sized, with dramatic black, white and red markings, this bird can be elusive. Frequently I encountered the substantial oblong holes it hammers out of dead trees, and sometimes heard its powerful drumming and its ringing cry. Too often I was looking the other way when others glimpsed it among the trees. I became obsessed by my failure to see it.

Then, one morning on a canoe trip, I was awakened by its drum roll right outside my tent. The bird was so close I could hear it picking and tearing at loosened chips. As I crouched by the open tent flap, I discovered a bewildering reluctance—I didn't really want to see the bird! Once I'd seen it, my quest would be over, and this magical creature would become just another bird I'd checked off my list. Yet it would have been too eccentric to have rejected this chance, so I focused attentively on the spot where yellow chips flew from behind an ancient pine.

Almost immediately there was silence. The bird was gone. I searched for almost an hour, without a sign. Instead, and for the first time, I saw a handsome Black-backed Woodpecker, patiently scaling the bark from a dying spruce. Since that morning I've encountered many Pileated Woodpeckers—and I love them still—but only twice have I again seen that elusive Black-backed with its yellow crown.

The excerpts in this section explore peculiar and unsettling discoveries. An apparently simple decision—such as going into the garden to better hear the exquisite song of a bird—can lead to a glimpse of eternity. A child encounters a deeply mysterious presence in the night; an author is led to an unwelcome recognition of how the earth perceives us.

For us, as for Wagner's Siegfried, birds can be guides on our personal quests, as well as the objects of them. But quests have always held an element of danger.

G.G.

XLIII

"Rather the flight of the bird passing and leaving no trace"

Rather the flight of the bird passing and leaving no trace
Than creatures passing, leaving tracks on the ground.
The bird goes by and forgets, which is as it should be.
The creature, no longer there, and so, perfectly useless,
Shows it was there—also perfectly useless.

Remembering betrays Nature,
Because yesterday's Nature is not Nature.
What's past is nothing and remembering is not seeing.

Fly, bird, fly away; teach me to disappear.

ALBERTO CAEIRO (1879–1915), Portugal

Yellow-Breasted Chat, M. Catesby (1679–1749), England

Œnanthe Americana.　　　　　　　　　*Solanum &c fl: purpureo.*

THE ALBATROSS

IN *In Patagonia* I SUGGESTED that the Albatross which hung
from the neck of the Ancient Mariner was not the Great
Wandering Albatross but a smaller black species: either the
Sooty Albatross or the Black-browed. The Sooty is the likelier
of the two. It is a streamlined bird that keeps to the open sea.
I think I saw one off the south-east coast of Tierra del Fuego.
The Black-browed is everywhere, in the Magellan Straight
and the Beagle Channel, and resembles a large Greater Black-
backed Gull.

On the south side of the Beagle Channel is the Chilean
island of Navarino, with its naval base at Puerto Wiliams. I
hoped to walk around the coast and get a glimpse of Hermit
Island, which is the breeding colony of the Black-browed
Albatross. The wind and the rain drove me back.

East of the naval base there is a row of shacks in which

Black-Eyebrowed Albatros, H.C. Richter (1821–1902), Germany

live the last of the Fuegian Indians—the Indians Darwin mistook for the "missing link." He compared their language to the "grunts of animals," being unaware that a young Fuegian spoke as many words as Shakespeare ever wrote.

Most of the Fuegians on Navarino are half-bloods. But I met one old man, Grandpa Felipe, who was said to be almost pure. He was a frail old man, mending his crab-gear. He had never been strong. He watched his wife die. And all his children die.

"It was the epidemics," he said—and whenever he said the word *epidemias*, it sounded as a mournful refrain.

The Fuegians were as skillful canoers as the Eskimoes.

A year and a half later, when *In Patagonia* was in press, I went to the island of Steepholm in the Bristol Channel. My companion was a naturalist in his eighties. The purpose of our visit was to see in flower the peony that is supposed to have been brought here as a medicinal herb by monks from the Mediterranean.

I told my friend the story of how, in the nineteenth century, a Black-browed Albatross had followed a ship north of the Equator. Its direction-finding mechanism had been thrown out of line. It had ended up on a rock in the Faroe Islands where it lived for thirty-odd years and was known as "The King of the Gannets." The Hon. Walter Rothschild made a pilgrimage to see it. Finally, it was shot, stuffed and put in the Copenhagen Museum.

"But there's a new Albatross," the old man said. "A female bird. She was on Bass Rock last year, and I think she's gone to Hermaness."

Hermaness, at the tip of Unst in Shetland, is the ultimate headland of the British Isles.

From my flat in London, I called Bobby Tullock, the Shetland ornithologist.

"Sure, she's on Hermaness. She's made a nest among the Gannets and she's sitting proud. Why don't you come and see her? You'll find her on the West Cliff. You can't miss her."

I looked at my watch. It was nine o'clock. I had time to get to King's Cross Station before the night train left for Aberdeen. I put on my boots and packed a bag.

There was a hold-up on the tube. I almost missed the train. I ran down the platform at the last minute. The sleeping-car attendant was a craggy white-haired Scot in a maroon uniform with a gold braid. Beside him stood a small dark-haired young man, waiting.

I was out of breath.

"Have you got a berth?" I asked.

"Aye," said the sleeping-car attendant. "If you don't mind sharing with that!"

He jerked his thumb at the little man.

"Of course not," I said.

The man jumped in the upper bunk. I tried to talk. I tried English, French, Italian, Greek. Useless. I tried Spanish and it worked. I should have guessed. He was a South American Indian.

"Where are you from," I asked.

"Chile."

"I have been in Chile. Whereabouts?"

"Punta Arenas."

Punta Arenas on the Straights of Magellan is the southernmost city in the world.

"I was there," I said.

"I come from Punta Arenas. But that is not my home. My home is Navarino Island."

"You must know Grandpa Felipe."

"*Es mi tio.* He is my uncle."

Having exceptional powers of balance, the young man and his brother found work in Punta Arenas as refuellers of the light-buoys at the entrance to the Magellan Straight. In any sea they would jump onto the buoy and insert the fuel nozzle. After the fall of Allende, the brother got a job with an American oil company, using his talent on off-shore rigs. The company sent him to the North Sea oil field. He had asked for his brother to join him. They would each earn £600 a week.

I told him I was travelling north to see a bird that had flown from his country. The story mystified him.

Two days later I lay on the West Cliff off Hermaness and watched the Albatross through binoculars: a black exception in a snow field of Gannets. She sat, head high and tail high, on her nest of mud, on her clutch of infertile eggs.

I too am mystified by the story.

BRUCE CHATWIN (1940–1989), England

A Taste of Paradise

STEVENSON SUDDENLY HAD THE IMPRESSION that many hours had passed since he had first entered the room with Mister Baker. Had his host been speaking just now? He couldn't tell. Next to the carafe, which was once again full, sat a plate of small fried fish which he had not noticed before, and their fixed black eyes appeared to him like the eyes of a single round creature, staring horribly at him from the middle of the table. What time was it? Somewhere, from a back room, came the ticking of a clock. Stevenson remembered the story of a monk who had been distracted from his copy-work by the song of a bird. He went into the garden to listen more closely, and when he returned, after what he thought were only a few minutes, he discovered that a century had gone by, that his fellow monks were dead and his ink had turned to dust. The song of the bird had given him a taste of Paradise, where an instant is as a hundred years of earthly time. Was the same true of time in hell, Stevenson asked himself.

ALBERTO MANGUEL (1948–), Argentina/Canada
from *Stevenson Under the Palm Trees*

Bird on tapa cloth folk art, artist unknown (contemporary), New Zealand

Woodstork, T. Jasper (19th century),
United States

FROM THE WIND-UP BIRD CHRONICLE

THE BOY HEARD the hard-edged sound in the middle of the night. He came awake, reached out for the floor lamp, and, once it was on, sat up and looked around the room. The time on the wall clock was just before two. The boy could not imagine what might be happening in the world at a time like this.

Then the sound came again—from outside the window, he was sure. It sounded like someone winding a huge spring. Who could be winding a spring in the middle of the night? No, wait: it was like someone winding a spring, but it was not really a spring. It was the cry of a bird. The boy carried a chair over to the window and climbed up onto it. He pulled the curtains back and opened the window a crack. In the middle of the sky hung a large white moon, the full moon of late autumn, filling the yard below with its light. The trees out there looked very different to the boy at night than they did in the daylight. They had none of their usual friendliness. The evergreen oak looked almost annoyed as it trembled in the occasional puff of wind with an unpleasant creaking sound. The stones in the garden looked whiter and smoother than they ordinarily did, staring up at the sky impassively like the faces of dead people.

The cry of the bird seemed to be coming from the pine tree. The boy leaned out the window and looked up, but from this low angle, the large, heavy branches of the pine hid the bird. He wanted to see what it looked like. He wanted to memorize its color and shape so that tomorrow he could find it in his illustrated encyclopedia. His intense desire to know had brought him fully awake now. Finding birds and fish and other animals in his encyclopedia was his greatest joy. Its big, thick volumes lined one shelf of his room. He had yet to enter elementary school, but he already knew how to read.

The bird fell silent after winding the spring several times in a row. The boy wondered whether anyone else had heard the cry. Had his father and mother heard it? His grandmother? If not, he could tell them all about it in the morning: a bird that sounded just like the winding of a spring was sitting in the pine tree last night at two o'clock. If only he could catch a glimpse of it! Then he could tell everybody its name.

But the bird never raised its cry again. It fell silent as a stone, up there in the branches of the pine bathed in moonlight. Soon a chill wind blew into the room, as if giving him some kind of warning. The boy shuddered and closed the window. This was a different kind of bird, he knew, not some sparrow or pigeon, which showed itself to people without hesitation. He had read in his encyclopedia that most nocturnal birds were cunning and cautious. The bird probably knew that he was on the lookout for it. It would never come out as long as he waited for it to appear. The boy wondered if he should go to the bathroom. That would mean walking down the long, dark corridor. No, he would just go back to bed. It was not so bad that he couldn't wait until morning.

The boy turned the light out and closed his eyes, but thoughts of the bird in the pine tree kept him awake. The bright moonlight spilled in from beneath the curtains as if in invitation. When the wind-up bird cried one more time, the boy leaped out of bed. This time he did not turn on the light, but slipping a cardigan over his pajamas, he climbed onto the chair by the window. Parting the curtains just the tiniest bit, he peered up into the pine tree. This way, the bird would not notice that he was there.

WHAT THE BOY saw this time, though, was the outline of two men. He caught his breath. The men knelt like two black shadows at the base of the pine tree. Both wore dark clothing. One had no hat on, the other wore what looked like a felt hat with a brim. Why are these strange men here in our garden in the middle of the night? the boy wondered. Why wasn't the dog barking at them? Maybe he ought to tell his parents right away. But his curiosity held him at the window. He wanted to see what the men were doing.

Then, without warning, the wind-up bird cried out again. More than once, it sent its long, creaking sound out into the night. But the men did not seem to notice. They never budged, never looked up. They remained kneeling at the base of the tree, face-to-face. They seemed to be discussing something in low tones, but with the branches blocking the moonlight, the boy could not make out their faces. Before long, the two men stood up at the same moment. There was a good eight-inch difference in their heights. Both men were thin, and the tall one (the one with the hat) wore a long coat. The short one had on more form-fitting clothes.

The shorter man approached the pine tree and stood there, looking up into the branches. After a while, he began patting and grabbing the trunk with both hands as if inspecting it, until, all at once, he jumped up onto it. Then, with no effort whatever (or so it seemed to the boy), he came zipping up the tree like a circus performer. The boy knew this tree like an old friend. He knew that climbing it was no easy feat. Its trunk was smooth and slippery, and there was nothing to hold on to until you got up fairly high. But why was the man climbing the tree in the middle of the night? Was he trying to catch the wind-up bird?

The tall man stood at the base of the tree, looking up. Soon after, the small man disappeared from view. The branches rustled now and then, which meant that he must still be climbing up the tall pine. The wind-up bird would be sure to hear him coming and fly away. The man might be good at climbing trees, but the wind-up bird would not be that easy to capture. If he was lucky, though, the boy was hoping he might be able to catch a glimpse of the wind-up bird as it took off. He held his breath, waiting for the sound of wings. But the sound of wings never came, nor was there any cry.

THERE WAS NO sound or movement for a very long time. Everything was bathed in the white, unreal light of the moon, the yard like the wet bottom of a sea from which the water has just been suddenly removed. Entranced, motionless, the boy went on staring at the pine tree and the tall man left behind. He could not have torn his eyes away if he had tried. His breath clouded the glass. Outdoors, it must be cold. The tall man stood looking up, hands on hips, never moving, as if he had frozen in place. The boy imagined that he was worried about his shorter companion, waiting for him to accomplish some mission and come climbing down out of the pine tree. Nor would it have been strange for the man to be worried: the boy knew that the tall tree was harder to climb down than up. But then, all of a sudden, the tall man stalked off into the night, as if abandoning the whole project.

The boy felt that now he was the only one left behind. The small man had disappeared into the pine tree, and the tall one had gone off somewhere. The wind-up bird maintained its silence. The boy wondered if he should wake his father. But he knew he could not get him to believe this. "I'm sure you just had another dream," his father would say. It was true, the boy did often dream, and he often mistook his dreams for reality, but he didn't care what anybody said: this was *real*—the wind-up bird and the two men in black. They had just disappeared all of a sudden, that was all. His father would believe him if he did a good job of explaining what had happened.

It was then that the boy realized: the small man looked a lot like his father. Of course, he was too short to be his father, but aside from that, he was exactly the same: the build, the movements. But no, his father could never climb a tree that way. He wasn't that agile or strong. The more he thought about it, the more confused the boy became.

The tall man came back to the base of the tree. Now he had something in his hands—a shovel and a large cloth bag. He set the bag down on the ground and started digging near the roots of the tree. The shovel cut into the earth with a sharp, clean sound. Now everybody was bound to wake up, the boy thought. It was such a big, clear sound!

But no one woke up. The man went on digging without a break, seemingly unconcerned that anyone might hear him. Though tall and thin, he was far more powerful than he looked, judging from the way he used that shovel. He worked steadily, without wasted motion. Once he had the size hole he wanted, the man leaned the shovel against the tree and stood there looking down. He never once looked up, as though he had forgotten all about the man who had climbed the tree. The only thing on his mind now was the hole, it seemed. The boy did not like this. *He* would have been worried about the man in the tree.

The boy could tell from the mound of earth the man had dug out that the hole itself was not very deep—maybe just up over his own knees. The man seemed satisfied with the shape and size of the hole. He turned to the bag and gently lifted a blackish, cloth-wrapped object from inside it. The way the man held it, it seemed soft and limp. Maybe the man was about to bury some kind of corpse in the hole. The thought made the boy's heart race. But the thing in the cloth was no bigger than a cat. If human, it could only be an infant. But why did he have to bury something like that in *my yard?* thought the boy. He swallowed the saliva that he had unconsciously allowed to collect in his mouth. The loud gulp he made frightened the boy himself. It might have been loud enough for the man to hear outside.

Just then, as if aroused by the boy's gulp, the wind-up bird cried out, winding an even bigger spring than before: *Creeeak. Creeeak.*

When he heard this cry, the boy felt intuitively that something very important was about to happen. He bit his lip and unconsciously scratched the skin of his arms. He should never have seen any of this, he felt. But now it was too late. Now it was impossible for him to tear his eyes away from the scene before him. He parted his lips and pressed his nose against the cold windowpane, transfixed by the strange drama that was now unfolding in his yard. He was no longer hoping for other members of the family to get out of bed. *No one would wake up anyway, no matter how big a sound they made out there. I'm the only person alive who can hear these sounds. It was that way from the start.*

HARUKI MURAKAMI (1949–), Japan

Horned Screamer, G.L. Leclerc, Comte de Buffon (1707–1788), France

THE HORNED SCREAMER.

VULTURES

Hung there in the thermal
whiteout of noon, dark ash
in the chimney's updraft, turning
slowly like a thumb pressed down
on target; indolent V's; flies, until they drop.

Then they're hyenas, raucous
around the kill, flapping their black
umbrellas, the feathered red-eyed widows
whose pot bodies violate mourning,
the snigger at funerals,
the burp at the wake.

They cluster, like beetles
laying their eggs on carrion,
gluttonous for a space, a little
territory of murder: food
and children.

Frowzy old saint, bald-
headed and musty, scrawny-
necked recluse on your pillar
of blazing air which is not
heaven: what do you make
of death, which you do not
cause, which you eat daily?

I make life, which is a prayer.
I make clean bones.
I make a gray zinc noise
which to me is a song.

Well, heart, out of all this
Carnage, could you do better?

MARGARET ATWOOD (1939–), Canada

Egyptian Vultures, F.O. Morris (1810–1893), Ireland/England

FROM A COMMONPLACE BOOK

In the time of the Saxon Heptarchie, in England, there was a King and Queene of Mercia, or the Mid-land, who were not onlie renowned, for their eminent Vertues and beautie, but more for their mutuall and inherent love. And to the King, who was a younge and active Prince, it seem'd not happiness enough, to enioy soe excellent a Queene, except he could also furnish himself of a friend, or favorite, to whom hee might trust and comunicate, his dearest, and most private affaires. It hapned, that not long after, rather by affection than Judgment, he lighted upon a Norman Gentleman named San' Foy; a man of a fair smiling outside, but who had nothing left within to make it good, but a fine flattery, and courtlie falsehood. Him this good king, not only took into his most privitt Counsille,

Sparrow, artist and country unknown

but divided with him all the Arcana of his Soule, and Sovraignetie; but more to bind him with favour: powr'd into him those secretts , which eft soone discuver'd his deprav'd nature. For as a Prince who had the power, to transforme himself, as often as he would, into anie other Creature, in the instant of time; and deading [sic] his own bodie, could make his Spirit live in another; Hee withdrew him one day into his Chamber, whither (among manie other privacies) he taking him by the hand, said San' Foy, I could show thee now a secret, which I never communicated with anie Soule, but my best beloved Queene, neither, till I saw thee, durst I ever imagine another brest worthie or capable of it; but thine, from whome I can hide nothing, though shalt receive it. This is it, observe and mark it. And therewith drawing forth of his pocket a Sparrow, having shutt all the doors, the king laid him selfe upon the floor, on his back, his face upwardes, and bade him fear nothing. Then stifling the bird, he putt the dead bill into his mouth, and breath'd upon it. Instantlie the King's bodie became cold, and a Carckasse, whilst the sparrow begun to pipp, and hopp about the Roome, and San' Foy amazed with the suddane revivall of the bird, now sitting on his head, then on his shoulder, then flying about the chamber chirping, then hopping upon his hand, at length returning to the dead king, returning to the dead king, and inserting his bill in his cold lippes, restored his borrowed Soule, and fill'd the emptie veines with the first spiritts. San' Foy, astonish'd at this Sight, humbly begg'd of the king the knowledge, and key of the Secrett. Hee as willing to grant as the other was to aske it, bade him lie down in the same manner as he saw him to do before, and giving him an herbe to chaw in his mouth, and laying another within his breast, held the dead Sparrow to his Mouth, and will'd him to breath thereon. San' Foy, fearlessly did it; when the bird began to take joy in his bold flight, five or six times about the roome, but at last returning to the Carckass of San' Foy, animated it again. That by daily participating, and gratifying this Secrett, he grew more and more in to the King's bosome, and under concealement of his owne to-be-abhorred Mischiefe, he putt on the Maske or Vizor of a most obsequious servant. For within he was soe possessed with the thirst of sovreigntie, and the lust of enjoying the Queene, his mistresse, but the onlie hope of his safetie, was to make good his trechrie, in the highest degree; and by a new varitie of Manners, and a confused temper of vices to come forth in one, and the same person, an appearing friend, and a most cruell enemie. See now, I pray you, whither the furious lust or the frantick desires of the Ambitious, will transport the guiltie?

FOLGER V. A. 241

Linguist Staff Finial (detail), Akan (Asante Kingdom) (20th century), Ghana

BLUE-BREAST

YOU PROBABLY, SOME OF YOU, never heard of the blue-breast; very few, certainly, have seen one alive, and, if alive, certainly not wild in England.

Here is a picture of it, daintily done, and you can see the pretty blue shield on its breast, perhaps, at this distance. Vain shield, if ever the fair little thing is wretched enough to set foot on English ground! I find the last that was seen was shot at Margate so long ago as 1842,—and there seems to be no official record of any visit before that, since Mr. Thomas Embledon shot one on Newcastle town moor in 1816. But this rarity of visit to us is strange; other birds have no such clear objection to being shot, and really seem to come to England expressly for the purpose. And yet this blue-bird—(one can't say "blue robin"—I think we shall have to call him "bluet," like the cornflower)—stays in Sweden, where it sings so sweetly that it is called "a hundred tongues."

Blue Throat, K. Svolinsky (1896–1986), Czech

11. That, then, is the utmost which the lords of land, and masters of science, do for us in their watch upon our feathered suppliants. One kills them, the other writes classifying epitaphs.

We have next to ask what the poets, painters, and monks have done.

The poets—among whom I affectionately and reverently class the sweet singers of the nursery, mothers and nurses—have done much; very nearly all that I care for your thinking of. The painters and monks, the one being so greatly under the influence of the other, we may for the present class together; and may almost sum their contributions to ornithology in saying that they have plucked the wings from birds, to make angels of men, and the claws from birds, to make devils of men.

If you were to take away from religious art these two great helps of its—I must say, on the whole, very feeble—imagination; if you were to take from it, I say, the power of putting wings on shoulders, and claws on fingers and toes, how wonderfully the sphere of its angelic and diabolic characters would be contracted! Reduced only to the sources of expression in face or movements, you might still find in good early sculpture very sufficient devils; but the best angels would resolve themselves, I think, into little more than, and not often into so much as, the likenesses of pretty women, with that grave and (I do not say it ironically) majestic expression which they put on, when, being very fond of their husbands and children, they seriously think either the one or the other have misbehaved themselves.

JOHN RUSKIN (1819–1900), England

FROM NAPLES 44

BY INVITATION OF Ingeniere Crespi, with whom I have been on good terms since the episode of the leakage of information over Anzio, I took part yesterday, Sunday, in a family expedition to collect funghi and salad plants, and to try our luck with the migrant birds at the Lago di Patria, some ten miles along the coast to the west of Naples. We went in two cars, the Ingeniere, his eighteen-year-old son, Andrea, and myself in one, and Signora Crespi, a nephew and his wife in the second. As Crespi and his son proposed to shoot duck—or failing that, anything that flew—they were fantastically dressed in green knickerbockers and Alpine hats. Signora Crespi wore a costume in Scotch tartan of a fierce design from Milan. She and her party were after mushrooms and

Water Rail, K. Svolinsky (1896–1986), Czech

greenstuff, and to avoid confusion between edible fungi and others of extreme similarity of appearance which are deadly, they had brought with them an enormous rolled-up coloured poster to be used in carrying on comparisons in the field.

We arrived at the lake in less than an hour, having passed other families already busy in the fields, cutting dandelions and stuffing them in paper bags. The report was that as there had been no duck-shooting last autumn in this area—which had been fought over as the Germans withdrew to the line of the Volturno—the sporting expectations were bright. Signora Crespi and party were left at the edge of a small pine wood where the nephew had already spotted glistening yellow toadstools, towards which they ran carrying their poster, and uttering cries of delight. The rest of us carried on a mile or so to the shores of the lake.

Here the prospects seemed dismal. We stood, Crespis holding their splendid guns, looking out over a surface of water that was as clean as a newly polished mirror. Another party of sportsmen mooched into sight on the far side of the lake, then disappeared again. A peasant came up and offered to show Crespi where edible frogs could be taken, but his offer was declined. The lake was bordered by sedge which Andrea was determined to investigate. He went off, returning in about an hour slimed to the knees in mud, and carrying a handful of feathers trailing green legs, which had once been a moorhen. This was success. Father and son hugged each other with delight. A moorhen wasn't a duck, but it was the next best thing.

Andrea cleaned up as best he could and we drove back to where we'd left the rest of the family, who'd done reasonably well with the fungi, with a fair collection scraped from tree-trunks or discovered—revealed by their startling colours—among the black rotting pine needles. There was a joyful outcry at the sight of the moorhen, and kisses and more hugs for Andrea from the womenfolk. After that the fungus-gatherers were deserted once again and we drove off over a sunken road to a particularly good position Crespi knew of. There were areas, he said—and this was one of them—where migrant birds seemed to pause and to hover, as if to get their bearings. He spoke of people who sometimes brought small trees with them, covered them with bird-lime, and stuck them into the ground here—sure of a good catch, although he personally saw not much fun or skill in the practice. His own favorite device was a piece of Heath-Robinson equipment carried in sections in the boot of the car. This, when assembled, looked like a model oil-derrick, with a rotating top encrusted with pieces of mirror set at different angles, which, when in motion flashed into the sky, attracted the curiosity of passing birds, and brought them within range.

This contraption was set up near an isolated bush, where it would be convenient for tired and inquisitive birds to alight. Strings attached to the rotating head were stretched back to where we crouched in the deep road in hiding behind the car, and were wound by Andrea over a bobbin to set the thing in motion. We were in the middle of a vast field with flowering spikes of asphodel thrusting up from the grass all round, and in the middle distance the blackened debris of a German half-track. Our first success was with a lark, drawn out of the sky as if by a magnet, and destroyed by Crespi's impeccable shot. There followed buntings, more larks, wheatears chats, blackcaps and five or six neat grey-green half-ounces of warbler, hardly any of them spoiled to the eye by the tiny, specially

Goldfinch, K. Svolinsky (1896–1986), Czech

prepared shot with which Crespi had filled his cartridges in preparation for this delicate slaughter. Although these birds must have hailed from the north, they all appeared slightly different from our English version of similar species. Only a local goldfinch, alighting on the bush with a burst of brief twittering song before extermination, was totally familiar.

The final bag was eighteen small corpses having a total weight perhaps of a pound. Crespi regarded this as success, and an excellent return for the expenditure in ammunition and effort. The passion for hunting, he said, could come even before the pursuit of love, and be equally remote from the balance sheets of gain or loss. Ferdinand of Naples had spent the equivalent of several million pounds on building his palace at Capodimonte just because this hill was on the route of migrating *beccafiche*—warblers of all kinds—and having finished the palace, a road to Naples had to be built at the cost of another million or two. It was estimated, said Crespi, that every warbler eaten by the royal sportsman cost the nation a thousand ducats.

We joined up with the rest of the family by the edge of the wood, picnicked off salami, mortadella and mozzarella cheese, the latter warranted to have been produced from the authentic milk of the buffaloes raised in the swamps of the Volturno, and which in appearance and vascular rubbery texture attempts to imitate the testicles of these beasts. After that, it was back to Naples, dizzy with success. It had been, as all agreed, an excellent day's sport. I delicately extricated myself from the invitation to dinner that evening.

NORMAN LEWIS (1908–2003), England

Courtesan Walking
(in Yoshi-wara quarter)

Seeing The Courtesan On Parade
One Loses Power To Resist
Like A Cuckoo Falling In Mid-Flight.

Okumura Masanobu
(1686–1764), Japan

*This poem alludes to the legend of the
hermit Kumeno Senin, who lost his
magical powers of flight when distracted
by the sight of the naked legs of a young
washerwoman.*

Courtesan Walking, O. Masanobu

PHALLOS BIRD

A RELATIVELY COMMON FIGURE in the erotic art on Attic vases, the phallos bird, with its erect penis for a head and neck, is usually accompanied by a woman. According to some, such images refer to a commonplace view of woman's wantonness, which is most alarmingly expressed by the blind seer, Teiresias, who opined that women enjoyed sex nine times more than men.

JOE MILK (1949–1980), Canada

An Athenian lady and her pet on an Anthenian vase (5th century BC), Greece

MEDITATIONS ON A SMALL BIRD'S SKULL

Trying to think inside
its idiom no knife and fork and no
memento mori: "skull"
clobbers this
lighter-than-air variation
on the egg. Whoever lived here deftly
entered anonymity:
membrane of bone,
koan you could sit and write inside and then
go out to a movie (Hitchcock's comedy
"The Birds") and then come home and
fall asleep and dream the rite of spring and then
wake up and forget. Everyone
who reads would like to be read, sometime,
by the music. I have read or dreamt
that indigo buntings in their nests
gaze into the stars and that the stars
gaze back into them,
mapping their language on each tiny roof.
Planetaria. This may be
the death of distance and its children.
If, like me,
you feel the urge to stick the sharp end
in your ear
(hoping for some
secret of the air)
be careful.
We are big and blunt and easily fooled and know few
of the fine points of translation.

DON McKAY (1942–), Canada

Le heron

La grue

coucououou quon entend
a La nuit de trois ou quatre
Lieux loins dans le foretou
au bord des rivieres

2

I Lost My Way in the Woods

WHEN THEY FIRST WENT out hunting, I lost my way in the woods, having followed a certain bird that seemed to me peculiar. It had a beak like that of a parrot, and was of the size of a hen. It was entirely yellow, except the head which was red, and the wings which were blue, and it flew by intervals like a partridge. The desire to kill it led me to pursue it from tree to tree for a very long time, until it flew away in good earnest. Thus losing all hope, I desired to retrace my steps, but found none of our hunters, who had been constantly getting ahead, and had reached the enclosure. While trying to overtake them, and going, as it seemed to me, straight to where the enclosure was, I found myself lost in the woods, going now on this side now on that, without being able to recognize my position. The night coming on, I was obliged to spend it at the foot of great tree, and in the morning set out and walked until three o'clock in the afternoon, when I came to a little pond of still water. Here I noticed some game,

An owl, a heron, and a crane from *Codex Canadiensis*,
L. Nicolas (1634–after 1698), France

which I pursued, killing three or four birds, which were very acceptable, since I had had nothing to eat. Unfortunately for me there had been no sunshine for three days, nothing but rain and cloudy weather, which increased my trouble. Tired and exhausted I prepared to rest myself and cook the birds in order to alleviate the hunger which I began painfully to feel, and which by God's favor was appeased.

When I had made my repast I began to consider what I should do, and to pray God to give me the will and courage to sustain patiently my misfortune if I should be obliged to remain abandoned in this forest without counsel or consolation except the Divine goodness and mercy, and at the same time to exert myself to return to our hunters. Thus committing all to His mercy I gathered up renewed courage going here and there all day, without perceiving any foot-print or path, except those of wild beasts, of which I generally saw a good number. I was obliged to pass here this night also. Unfortunately I had forgotten to bring with me a small compass which would have put me on the right road, or nearly so.

SAMUEL DE CHAMPLAIN (1567–1635), France/Canada
from *Voyages of Samuel de Champlain (1611–1618)*

Sandhill Crane,
Reports of Explorations
and Surveys (1853–56),
United States

FROM THE AGONY OF FLIES

WHEN THE BIRDS FLOCK together to fly to Africa,
they dance. Their rhythms, fuller and more subtle
than our own, are born in the beating of their wings.
They do not stomp the ground, but gently beat the air,
which is well disposed to them. We, on the other hand,
are hated by the earth.

ELIAS CANETTI (1905–1994),
Bulgaria / Austria / England

And the fear of you and the dread of you shall be upon every beast of the earth, and upon every fowl of the air, upon all that moveth upon the earth, and upon all the fishes of the sea; into your hand are they delivered.

Every moving thing that liveth shall be meat for you; even as the green herb I have given you all things.

GENESIS 9.2.3

A Robin Redbreast in a cage
Sets all Heaven in a rage.

WILLIAM BLAKE

VII ~

A BIRD IN THE HAND

Birds we use, eat, wear and sell

Cook-Shop Proprietor's Costume, N. de Larmessin (1640–1725), France

IF YOU GET TO THEM at the right time of year, many birds are easy to catch. For an agile hunter, a small boy for example, there isn't much of a problem in collecting eggs and chicks from the nest; some adults can also be snatched by hand. Commercial hunters in the nineteenth century reported that Passenger Pigeons—once their eggs had hatched—could be plucked right off the nest, "easy as spit," as one of them said. "They wouldn't even blink." The geese and ducks that undergo an annual flightless replacement of feathers—the moult—must always have provided humans with food, and sometimes with clothing or ritual decorations.

However, we've thought up many other uses for birds, the majority of them cruel. We've run cockfights, flown hawks and falcons in the hunt, kept caged birds for their songs and colours; we've employed canaries in mines and for magic tricks, and we've bred homing pigeons for war and sport.

The exploitation of birds can be as simple as keeping a demented budgerigar in a cage, or stuffing a turkey at Christmas: it can also be astonishingly ostentatious, as were the expeditions of the Grand Khan—described by Marco Polo—which could involve "ten thousand falconers, who carry with them a vast number of gerfalcons, peregrine falcons, and sakers, as well as many vultures, in order to pursue the game."

There is still a huge black market in falcons. A female White-phase Gyrfalcon will sell for well over 50,000 USD. The rarer a thing is, the more a collector is willing to pay. Because so many exotic species are now threatened—with many on the edge of extinction—the trade in birds becomes ever more lucrative. The highest black market price paid for a Lears Macaw, of which there are fewer than 160 left in the wild, is £120,000 (230,250 USD or 285,351 CAN). Birds of Paradise, rare owls and parrots also bring in big money. Their eggs do, as well. In the early 1980s a lovely and delicate Ross' Gull, one of the first to nest in North America, had her eggs stolen from beneath her.

Even among birdwatchers there are those who feel the need to possess the birds, if only symbolically. On a brisk day among the cognoscenti you can hear voices calling out, "What have you got? Have you got the Prothonotary, the Lazuli Bunting, the Merlin?" Or whatever the local rarity might be. To have them is to tick them off on your list. And the best list is the "life list"—the record of all the species you have ever seen.

I must here confess that Harold Wilson, my Mexican parrot, was purchased illegally. He was in the bottom of a burlap sack carried by an impoverished Zapotec Indian kid, and when I saw his wretched state I bought him; God knows what would have happened to him if I hadn't, but I'm afraid that wasn't my only reason. I'd always wanted a parrot, ever since reading *Treasure Island*.

What is it, this urge to own another living creature? And why is it that we understand so well the universal symbol of the bird being set free from a cage?

It's we who have made the cages. It's we who must open them.

G.G.

THE MOUNTAIN KIWI

I HAVE VERY LITTLE TO SAY regarding this bird, as I have only seen two of them, and being pushed with hunger, I ate the pair of them, under the circumstances I would have eaten the last of the Dodos.

It is all very well for science, lifting up its hands in horror, at what I once heard called gluttony, but let science tramp through the Westland bush or swamps, for two or three days without food, and find out what hunger is. Besides at the time, which was many years ago, I was not aware that it was an almost extinct bird. Had I known so, I would at least have skinned it and kept the head and feet.

CHARLES EDWARD DOUGLAS (1840–1916),
Scotland/New Zealand

HE IS THEN DELICIOUS, ROASTED

THE GRASS GROWS THICK and green, drawing its nourishment from the earth. The Locust crops it. The Mantis makes a meal of the Locust and swells out with eggs, which are laid, in three batches, to the number of a thousand. When they hatch, up comes the Ant and levies an enormous tribute on the brood. We appear to be retroceding. In vastness of bulk, yes; in refinement of instinct, certainly not. In this respect how far superior is the Ant to the Mantis! Besides, the cycle of possible happenings is not closed.

Young Ants still contained in their cocoon—popularly known as Ants'-eggs—form the food on which the Pheasant's

ABOVE: *Wryneck,* K. Svolinsky (1896–1986), Czech
OPPOSITE: North Island Brown Kiwi in nest burrow with egg, R. Morris (contemporary), New Zealand

brood is reared. These are domestic poultry just as much as the Pullet and the Capon, but their keep makes greater demands on the owner's care and purse. When it grows big, this poultry is let loose in the woods; and people calling themselves civilized take the greatest pleasure in bringing down with their guns the poor creatures which have lost the instinct of self-preservation in the pheasantries, or, to speak plainly, in the poultry-yard. You cut the throat of the chicken required for roasting; you shoot, with all the parade of sport, that other Chicken, the Pheasant. I fail to understand those insensate massacres.

Tartarin of Tarascon, in the absence of game, used to shoot at his cap. I prefer that. And above all I prefer the hunting, real hunting, of another fervent consumer of Ants, the Wryneck, the *Tiro-lengo* of the Provençaux, so-called because of his scientific method of darting his immensely-long and sticky tongue across a procession of Ants and then suddenly withdrawing it all black with the limed insects. With such mouthfuls as these, the Wryneck becomes disgracefully fat in autumn; he plasters himself with butter on his rump and sides under the wings; he hangs a string of it round his neck; he pads his skull with it right down to the beak.

He is then delicious, roasted: small, I admit; no bigger than a Lark, at the outside; but, small though he be, unlike anything else and immeasurably superior to the Pheasant, who must begin to go bad before developing a flavour at all.

J. Henri Fabre (1823–1915), France

from Into the Heart of Borneo

THE NIGHT BEFORE we were due to leave, Leon called to take us to Dana's longhouse. He was becoming less shy and awkward and, when Bidai and Siba and Edward were not about, he was prepared to talk in English. As we left the hotel and walked up the hill he drew me aside.

"Redmon," he said, sotto voce, "I hopes you and Jams not go with hotel girls?"

"I haven't seen any hotel girls."

"They on top floor. Very naughties."

"Do you go with hotel girls?"

"No Redmon," said Leon, with great seriousness, "there is new diseases here. Your spear it rots. You go to hospital, they look at your spear, you take medicine. We have a word for this diseases. I not know it in English. We Iban, in our language, we call it syphilis."

The road wound up out of the town, past a small airstrip and a group of government houses and into secondary jungle. We turned off on to a footpath which curved along the sides of a series of small hills. I carried a kit-bag containing presents for Dana: two bottles of whisky, an outsize pipe made in London, a tin of Balkan Sobranie, and my cartridge belt. This last, an English, old, hand-sewn, worn, and desirable cartridge belt, I was parting with under protest ("But Redmond," James had said, "what possible use could it be now you've been disarmed? What do you mean—it's a lucky cartridge belt, you've shot lots of pheasants with it? Redmond, you are an Ignoble Savage.").

The jungle around us was secondary jungle, a re-growth of thick vegetation, of tangled young trees and bushes and creepers on ground that had been felled, burned and cleared for a season's crop of hill padi perhaps ten or fifteen years ago. Rounding a bend on the path, we found ourselves staring straight at a raven-sized bird with a deep chestnut-coloured back, a hooked beak, a red eye and a long black tail. It hopped off the branch of a small tree, flapped twice and floated, its wings outstretched, its legs hanging, across a small clearing and into dense bushes where it disappeared from view.

"What the hell was that, Leon?" I said.

"Bubut," said Leon. "He is a friend to the Iban. We leave him alone. He helps us grow padi. He eat all the insect."

When I looked up the Chestnut-raven-glider in Smythies, later, there was no possibility of mistaking such a forceful identity: it was a Common coucal, Centropus sinesis, a cuckoo that builds its own nest, a good, honest, "bulky ball of grass with the entrance at the side." In the coucal's case, however, it might have been wiser to put one's eggs in other people's incubation baskets, because in Sabah the young of both this and the Lesser Coucal are used medicinally by natives and Chinese alike. When they locate a nest they keep a very close watch upon it until the chicks are hatched and then, a day or two later, they break the legs of the chicks. They believe that upon finding the chicks injured the parent birds forage for healing herbs which they half-digest and then regurgitate to use as a dressing on the limbs. The legs quickly heal and mend, and the goodness of the medicine is (they believe) retained in the blood of the chicks. The procedure may be repeated and often the chicks are hand fed with cooked rice for a few days before being collected and bottled whole in brandy or other spirit. The resulting liquid is used both internally and externally as a cure-all, especially for rheumatic complaints.

REDMOND O'HANLON (1947–), England

Greater Coucal, S. Parkinson (c.1745–1771), Scotland

The Raven-Tree

On the Blackmoor estate there is a small wood called Losel's, of a few acres, that was lately furnished with a set of oaks of a peculiar growth and great value; they were tall and taper like firs, but standing near together had very small heads, only a little brush without any large limbs. About twenty years ago the bridge at the Toy, near Hampton-court, being much decayed, some trees were wanted for the repairs that were fifty feet long without bough, and would measure twelve inches diameter at the little end. Twenty such trees did a purveyor find in this little wood, with this advantage, that many of them answered the description at sixty feet. These trees were sold for twenty pounds apiece.

In the centre of this grove there stood an oak, which, though shapely and tall on the whole, bulged out into a large excrescence about the middle of the stem. On this a pair of ravens had fixed their residence for such a series of years, that the oak was distinguished by the title of the Raven-tree. Many were the attempts of the neighbouring youths to get at this eyry: the difficulty whetted their inclinations, and each was ambitious of surmounting the arduous task. But, when they arrived at the swelling, it jutted out so in their way, and was so far beyond their grasp, that the most daring lads were awed, and acknowledged the undertaking to be too hazardous. So the ravens built on, nest upon nest, in perfect security, till the fatal day arrived in which the wood was to be levelled. It was in the month of February, when those birds usually sit. The saw was applied to the butt, the wedges were inserted into the opening, the woods echoed to the heavy blows of the beetle or mallet, the tree nodded to its fall; but still the dam sat on. At last, when it gave way, the bird was flung from her nest; and, though her parental affection deserved a better fate, was whipped down by the twigs, which brought her dead to the ground.

GILBERT WHITE (1720–1793), England

The Only Good Law

NOTHING MARKED MORE CLEARLY the growing power of squirearchy in the House of Commons and in the State than the Game Laws of the Restoration period. By the Forest Laws of Norman and Plantagenet times, the interests of all classes of subjects had been sacrificed in order that the King should have abundance of red deer to hunt; but now the interests of the yeomen and farmers were sacrificed in order that the squire should have plenty of partridges to shoot. Even more than politics, partridges caused neighbours to look at one another askance: for the yeoman freeholder killed, upon his own little farm, the game that wandered over it from the surrounding estates of game preservers. And so in 1671 the Cavalier Parliament passed a law which prevented all freeholders of under a hundred pounds a year—that is to say the very great majority of the class—from killing game, even on their own land. Thus many poor families were robbed of many good meals that were theirs by right; and even those few yeoman whose wealth raised them above the reach of this remarkable law, were for that reason regarded with suspicion. The best that even the good-hearted Sir Roger de Coverley can bring himself to say of the 'yeoman of about a hundred pounds a year,' 'who is just within the Game Act,' is that 'he would make a good neighbour if he did not destroy so many partridges'—that is to say upon his own land.

For many generations to come, grave social consequences were to flow from the excessive eagerness of the country gentlemen about the preservation of game. Their anxieties on that score had grown with the adoption of the shot-gun. During the Stuart epoch shooting gradually superseded hawking, with the result that birds were more rapidly destroyed, and the supply no longer seemed inexhaustible. In Charles II's reign it was already not unusual to 'shoot flying.' But it was regarded as a difficult art, the more so as it was sometimes practised from horseback. But the 'perching' of pheasants by stalking and shooting them as they sat on the boughs, was still customary among gentleman. [See § 106, 107, 108.]

The netting of birds on the ground was a fashionable sport, often carried on over dogs who pointed the game concealed in the grass. [See § 109.] It is written that Sir Roger 'in his youthful days had taken forty coveys of partridges in a season' probably by this means. To lure wild duck, by the score and the hundred, into a decoy upon the water's edge was a trade in the fens and a sport on the decoy-pond of the manor-house. Liming by twigs, snaring and trapping birds of all kinds, not only pheasants and wild duck but thrushes and fieldfares, had still a prominent place in manuals of *The Gentleman's Recreation*. But the shot-gun was clearly in the ascendant, and with it the tendency to confine sport more and more to the pursuit of certain birds specifically listed as *game*. In that sacred category a place had recently been granted by Statute to grouse and blackcock; already the heather and bracken where they lurked were protected from being burnt except at certain times of the year, and the shepherd transgressing the law was liable to be whipped. Addison's Tory squire declared the new Game Law to be the only good law passed since the Revolution.

G.M. TREVELYAN (1876–1962), England
from *Illustrated English Social History*

Only Child

The early conflict made him pale
and when he woke from those long weeping slumbers she was
        there

and the air about them—hers and his—
sometimes a comfort to him, like a quilt, but more
often than not a fear.

There were times he went away—he knew not where—
over the fields or scuffing to the shore;
suffered her eagerness on his return
for news of him—where had he been, what done?
He hardly knew, nor did he wish to know
or think about it vocally or share
his private world with her.

Then they would plan another walk, a long
adventure in the country, for her sake—
in search of birds. Perhaps they'd find the blue
heron today, for sure the kittiwake.

Birds were familiar to him now, he knew
them by their feathers and a shyness like his own
soft in the silence.
Of the ducks she said, "Observe,
the canvas back's a diver," and her words
stuccoed the slatey water of the lake.

He had no wish to separate them in groups
or learn the latin,
or, waking early to their song remark, "the thrush,"
or say at evening when the air is streaked
with certain swerving flying,
"Ah, the swifts."

Birds were his element like air and not
her words for them—making them statues
setting them apart,
nor were they facts and details like a book.
When she said, "Look!"
he let his eyeballs harden
and when two came and nested in the garden
he felt their softness, gentle, near his heart.

She gave him pictures which he avoided, showing
strange species flat against a foreign land.
Rather would he lie in the grass, the deep grass of the island
close to the gulls' nests knowing
these things he loved and needed near his hand,
untouched and hardly seen but deeply understood.
Or sail among them through a wet wind feeling
their wings within his blood.

Like every mother's boy he loved and hated
smudging the future photograph she had,
yet struggled within the frames of her eyes and then
froze for her, the noted naturalist—
her very affectionate and famous son.
But when most surely in her grasp, his smile
darting and enfolding her, his words:
"Without my mother's help . . ." the dream occurred.

Dozens of flying things surrounded him
on a green terrace in the sun
and one by one
as if he held caresses in his palm
he caught them all and snapped and wrung their necks
brittle as little sticks.

Then through the bald, unfeathered air
and coldly as a man would walk
against a metal backdrop, he
bore down on her
and placed them in her wide maternal lap
and accurately said their names aloud:
woodpecker, sparrow, meadowlark, nuthatch.

P.K. PAGE (1916–), England/Canada

Fiery Topaz,
H.C. Richter (1821–1902),
England

The Hatters and Dressmakers
of Europe

But the reckless Elisée Reclus in his *Nouvelle Géographie Universelle*, of 1893, declares that the bird population of Trinidad once amounted to ¾ of that of all of Europe which, considering that Trinidad is about the size of Lancashire, is a bewildering thought. But mankind has wrought terrible carnage among them. The chief victims were the hummingbirds after which, in pre-Columbian times, the Caribs baptized the Island. No less than fifteen thousand of these little creatures, M. Reclus states, were stuffed and exported weekly to the hatters and dressmakers of Europe; and when one thinks of the fashions of the 'nineties and of the pictures of Boldini and Helleu, and of the old hats that one still comes across in cupboards, the number of these posthumous migrants hardly seems exaggerated.

Patrick Leigh Fermor (1915–), England

A Terrified Mass of Birds

Dark as thunderclouds, each morning a roar of wings filled the sky as the males returned to the eggs, to the females who sprang hungrily into the air, so that spiralling funnels rose and fell on every hand. It remained magnificent and terrifying; a marvel they never collided; a mystery that in those roiling millions, each found its own nest, its own mate, that the female seemed to recognize the sound of his wingbeat. Before the male arrived, she sprang wildly into the air and was gone even as he touched down.

And so they alternated, brooding and eating, eating and brooding, while hunters slaughtered them on the feeding grounds. . . .

Convinced the birds would return like this each year, that there was some key that would make him a fortune, Robert searched out men like Silas Wilder. He demanded to know how many eggs, how many in the hatch, how long the incubation and what the birds ate, how long they lived and where they went in summer, in winter, the best baits and traps. He watched men stringing seine nets over rivers where low-flying birds would strike them and become hopelessly entangled or tumble into the water to be collected downstream by the men in boats or on rafts. He helped set up a purse net thirty paces wide at the opening and four times the height of a man, which narrowed to the size of a sock, so that great flocks, entering at full flight, were tumbled together, a terrified mass of birds the men could set upon and dispatch with ease.

Passenger Pigeons, artist and dates unknown

"I tell you, sir, I had to work and work hard." With a face like old leather, his head completely bald but the rest of his body covered with hair, Silas Wilder imprisoned a male bird under his belly and between his thighs. "If I had my memory, I could tell you of lots like me, ordinary men who knew what work meant." Crippled by running an ox team in winter, as he'd tell anyone, in water like as not, pulling timber for the Baron (a bastard right enough, he wouldn't drag a soldier off his mother), Silas must have been eighty-five if he was a day. "Like what's-his-name," blinking vacantly, "a mate of mine, gunner for the government in '37, he had his leg shot off." Taking the bird's head between thumb and curled forefinger, he clamped his good leg against the lame one. "Easy, you bastard, easy!" He held the bird steady, sewing one eyelid shut and then the other. "He called to see the mangled limb. What was his name? Gave three cheers for the Queen and died."

Silas wiped the blood from the bird's face with the heel of his hand, then strapped both red legs to a willow stick. Raising it aloft, he dropped his arm once, twice; and each time the bird, a fine-looking creature over a foot and a half long, beat its wings in alarm. "There," said the old man, "that'll fool them." Laying bird and stick on the ground, he belched happily. "Aubrey! His name was Aubrey Wilson. . . ."

With bulging eyes, his mouth pursed like a small red button, he stared at Robert. Behind him several men propped dead pigeons to look as if they were dozing in the sun. "Tell me, sir . . ." Retrieving his stick, so the pigeon exploded in a blind flurry of wings, of grunting chirps, he struggled to his feet. . . .

There was a chorus of whispers. "Silas, for Chrissakes!" The men darted for cover because a dark cloud was rising in the north. "They're coming . . ." The old man scuttled to the anchor stick, secured the stool with its captive bird and then a cord to its other end.

Robert Fraser settled himself so he could view the edge of the bog, the open space ringed by spectral paper birch and poplar, moon trees reflecting light where others absorbed it— and above them now a good-sized flight of several thousand males. They swooped towards the clearing and over the eight men crouched unmoving, breathless, until Silas Wilder placed a reed contraption to his lips and blew a raspy drawn-out note, the enticing call of a feeding pigeon. Jerking the cord, he caused the willow to drop suddenly beneath the decoy male, so that leaping to maintain balance, with blindly flapping wings, he seemed to be calling to his fellows in the air. With suspicions now allayed, they descended to feed upon the salt.

When most of the birds had settled, a wee Frenchman at the end sprang the trap. There was a fierce collective cry of alarm, but too late. Huge wings enclosed them like a mouth, and while a few stragglers escaped, the men sprang quickly to their feet with loaded shotguns. "Huzzah, you bastards . . ." Of the two thousand males enticed into the clearing, not more than a hundred and fifty escaped. "G'wan and tell your mates about Silas Wilder and his crew," cried the hunters. "G'wan, g'wan!" Still waving their arms, stamping and bellowing, they approached the net which resembled a pudding about to burst. Grabbing the shrieking heads poking through the mesh, they silenced each skull between thumb and forefinger or severed it with tinsmiths' pincers.

GRAEME GIBSON (1934–), Canada
from *Perpetual Motion*

FEATHERED CAPES

THE INDIGENOUS PEOPLE also took their toll on the native birds. The spectacular feathered capes and helmets that became uniforms of rank among Hawaiian chiefs, and the ceremonial feather-garments known as *kahilis* (loosely translated, "fly flaps"), cost thousands of avian lives. During early periods of Hawaiian history, commoners were even obliged to pay tribute to their *alii* in the currency of feathers. Shiny black plumage from one species, scarlet from another, green from another. Yellow was the most valued color, a stroke of bad luck for species like *Drepanis pacifica*, the Hawaii *mamo*, with its bright yellow rump highlighted against a starling-black body. The annals of Hawaiian fashion tell us that one chief, Kamehameha the Great, possessed a resplendent yellow cape containing the feathers of eighty thousand *mamo*.

DAVID QUAMMEN (1948–), United States

Mamo, J.G. Keulemans (1842–1912), Netherlands/England

Asif of Laysan etc

DIOMEDEA IMMUTABILIS, ROTHSCH

WITH A TRECHEROUS HOOK AND LINE

FROM EARLY ON, albatrosses saved the lives of many Western mariners—albeit involuntarily. In 1881 a sailor who fell overboard from the ship *Gladstone* grabbed the first albatross that approached him and used it as a living life-buoy to stay afloat until the ship stopped, lowered a lifeboat, and rescued him. Castaways shipwrecked where few vessels ventured survived largely on albatrosses, sometimes for years. One gang of sealers was marooned on Solander Islands, south of New Zealand, from 1808 to 1813. Four men put ashore against their will on the Snares Islands in 1810 (48°S, 166°E) did not see another ship for seven years. Albatrosses helped feed them.

Laysan Albatross, J.G. Keulemans (1842–1912), Netherlands/England

When the sealer *Princess of Wales* wrecked on Île de la Possession in 1821, stranding its men for a year, Wandering Albatrosses kept them alive: "Their eggs are very large . . . about a pint. . . . The young . . . excellent for the table, and provided us with a very good dish for a long period, as they did not fly off until December." In 1842 the whaler *Parker* struck Kure Atoll's reef, and in the seven months until rescue, surviving men killed seven thousand seabirds and sixty Monk Seals. In what was surely the first conservation edict in the Northwestern Hawaiian Islands, the captain of the *Saginaw*, which in 1870 also went aground on Kure, limited his crew to twenty birds per day.

In 1875 a woman named Florence Wordsworth was bound from London to New Zealand aboard the *Strathmore* when it wrecked on the Isles of the Apostles in the southern Indian Ocean's Crozet group, drowning nearly half the passengers. She wrote, "I was stunned with cold, and almost fainting . . . till Charlie came with the reeking-hot skins of two albatrosses." During seven months on the island, until they were rescued by an American whaler, they ate birds. After killing an albatross, one of the men wrote, "As is often the case before dying, it vomited up the contents of its bag, and amongst the mess was an eel quite perfect, having the appearance of being cooked. I took it and ate it, and it tasted quite like stewed eel."

In 1916, after drifting sea ice clenched and later crushed his ship *Endurance*, Ernest Shackleton and five companions made landfall at South Georgia Island after a desperate eight-hundred-mile, gale-plagued lifeboat trek to summon rescuers for their marooned crew. "There we found the nests of albatrosses. . . . The nestlings were fat and lusty, and we had no hesitation about deciding that they were destined to die at an early age . . . what a stew it was. . . . The young albatrosses weighed about fourteen pounds each fresh killed. . . . The flesh was white and succulent, and the bones, not fully formed, almost melted in our mouths."

You didn't have to be shipwrecked to develop a taste for the great seabirds. On Captain James Cook's second circum-navigation, in 1772, naturalist George Forster noted both their beauty and their utility: "They skim always on the surface of the sea. . . . When skinned, they afford a good palatable food." George's father, Reinhold, added, "We found them to be extremely curious . . . but they paid with their lives for this curiosity." Cook himself wrote, "Shot some albatrosses and other Birds on which we feasted . . . and found them exceed-ing good." Another of Cook's naturalists, Joseph Banks, com-mented that the men "eat heartily of them tho there was fresh pork upon the table."

Explorers and sailors and, later, passengers on commer-cial ships learned early to catch albatrosses for their own craft-work, food, or amusement. Sealers and whalers made pipe stems of the long, hollow wing bones, tobacco pouches of the big webbed feet; and warm slippers from the downy skins. The egg occasionally found in females at sea was sometimes reserved for ships' captains.

Herman Melville, in *Moby-Dick*, had this impression:

I remember the first albatross I ever saw. It was during a prolonged gale, in waters hard upon the Antarctic seas. From my forenoon watch below, I ascended to the over-clouded deck; and there, dashed upon the main hatches, I saw a regal, feathery thing of unspotted whiteness. . . .

At intervals, it arched forth its vast archangel wings, as if to embrace some holy ark. Wondrous flutterings and throbbings shook it. . . . It uttered cries, as some king's ghost in supernatural distress. Through its inexpressible, strange eyes, methought I peeped to secrets which took hold of God. . . . I bowed myself; the white thing was so white, its wings so wide, and in those for ever exiled waters, I had lost the miserable warping memories of traditions and of towns. Long I gazed at that prodigy of plumage. . . . How had the mystic thing been caught? Whisper it not, and I will tell; with a treacherous hook and line.

CARL SAFINA (1955–), United States
from *Eye of the Albatross*

GOOSE GREASE

THE FAT OF MOST FOWLS is soft in texture, yellow or white (stearin and elain, in varied proportion), and it all melts easily. Goose fat being the softest (liquid at 111° F.) is always called goose grease; Turkey fat is more like chicken (melting point 113° F.); while Duck fat melts at 126° F. From these figures you realise why duck, roasted, needs a quick strong heat "to start it", compared with goose or turkey.

Goose grease is always treasured by country people as very useful. Well beaten to a cream, with vinegar, lemon juice, finely chopped onion, and chopped parsley, it is used as a filling for sandwiches. It is more appetising than it sounds, having the creamy white consistency of thick mayonnaise. Where the more sturdy Teuton element has remained in Britain, it is eaten on bread, seasoned only with salt and pepper.

In most farmhouses some goose grease is kept in the medicine chest and used in many ways. The old-fashioned hot poultice, so useful in relieving an old person's bronchitis, or easing the "tight chest" of a child, is temporarily out of hospital fashion. Poultices do entail trouble and care, both in application and in easing them away, and substituting warm flannel to guard against chill—but they serve a useful purpose, especially in the country, and many a doctor, long delayed by snow or distance, has arrived to find pneumonia averted, a warmed and soothed child placidly asleep. For any fomentation, goose grease, being water-proof, is rubbed on to the skin beforehand, to prevent the moist heat unduly soaking the skin, and a little is often added to the linseed for the same reason.

Goose grease and fine lard are the only creams permitted in the dairy, both for the dairymaids' hands and the churn fitments. It is also used, in east winds or snow, to anoint the udders of cows to prevent chapping. It was used by mothers with babies for the same reason, and later when children had colds in the head, noses and lips were rubbed with goose grease, before going out into the cold.

Goose grease is also used to soften stored leather, old straps, harness, shoes, etc., or suitcases and bags were smeared with goose grease (or neat's-foot oil) and left to stand in a warm room overnight, before being rubbed soft with dubbin or washed with saddle soap.

Goose grease, melted, beaten full of yellow broom and gorse flowers, and strained, made a yellow ointment much approved for skin trouble of man and beast. A green version, made with watercress juice was more liked by the sailors and fisherfolk (see Cress). Both ointments probably had real value, combined with the treatment of washing and fomentation. Goose grease, melted with horse-radish juice, mustard, and turpentine, and shaken till white and creamy, made embrocation for stiffness and rheumatism. Another form was emulsified with yolk of egg, or Irish moss solutions.

Warm goose grease gently smeared into the sheep-dog's ears, and between his pads, helped him through long days out in wet snow.

Finally goose grease was good in the stable for cracked hoofs, and was also much used by proud poultry-keepers, waggoners, and shepherds, to polish the beaks, legs, hoofs, or trotters of any animals going on show. It improved the texture of the translucent horn, and showed up its natural colour.

DOROTHY HARTLEY (1892–1985), England

Brandt's Cormorant, Reports of Expeditions and Surveys (1853–56), United States

Who First Devised to Cram Hens

They of the Island Delos began the cramming of Hens and Pullein first. And from them arose that detestable gourmandise and gluttonie to eat Hens and Capons so fat and enterlarded with their owne grease. Among the old statutes ordained for to represse inordinate feasts, I find in one act made by *C. Fannius*, a Consul of Rome, eleven yeres before the third Punick war, an expresse prohibition and restraint, That no man should have his table served with any foule, unlesse it were one hen, and no more, and the same a runner only, and not fed up and crammed fat. The branch of this statute was afterwards taken forth and inserted in al other acts provided in that behalfe, and went currant thorough all. Howbeit, for all the law so well set down, there was a starting hole found to delude and escape the meaning therof, namely, to feed Cocks and Capons also with a past soked in milk and mead together, for to make their flesh more tender, delicate, and of sweeter tast: for that the letter of the statute reached no farther than to Hens or Pullets.

As for the Hens, they only be thought good and well ynough cramm'd, which are fat about the neck, and have their skin plumpe and soft there. Howbeit, afterwards our fine cookes began to looke to their hind-parts about the rumpe, and chuse them thereby. And that they should make a greater shew in the platter, they slit them along the chine: and lay their legs out at large, that they might take up the whole dresser bourd. The Parthians also have taught our cooks their own fashions. And yet for all this fine dressing and setting out of meat, there is nothing that pleaseth and contenteth the tooth of man in all respects; while one loves nothing but the leg, another likes and praises the white brawne alone, about the breast bone.

The first that devised a Barton & Mue to keepe foule in, was *M. Laenius Strabo*, a gentleman of Rome, who made such an one at Brindisi, where he had enclosed birds of all kinds. And by his example we began to keepe foules within narrow coups and cages as prisoners, to which creatures Nature had allowed the wide aire for their scope and habitation.

PLINY THE ELDER (23–79), Rome

FROM READING LOLITA IN TEHRAN

"YES, DON'T YOU REMEMBER? I told my father I was translating Islamic texts into English to help Mahshid."

"But I thought that was just an excuse so that you could come here," I said.

"It was, but I decided to do these translations for at least three hours a week, sometimes more, for the extra lies. I reached a compromise with my conscience," she said with a smile.

"I have to tell you that the Ayatollah himself was no novice in sexual matters," Nassrin went on. "I've been translating his magnum opus, *The Political, Philosophical, Social and Religious Principles of Ayatollah Khomeini*, and he has some interesting points to make."

"But it's already been translated," said Manna. "What's the point?"

Folk art rooster, artist unknown (contemporary), Canada

258

"Yes," said Nassrin, "parts of it have been translated, but after it became the butt of party jokes, ever since the embassies abroad found out that people were reading the book not for their edification but for fun, the translations have been very hard to find. And anyway, my translation is thorough—it has references and cross-references to works by other worthies. Did you know that one way to cure a man's sexual appetites is by having sex with animals? And then there's the problem of sex with chickens. You have to ask yourself if a man who has had sex with a chicken can then eat the chicken afterwards. Our leader has provided us with an answer: *No*, neither he nor his immediate family or next-door neighbors can eat of that chicken's meat, but it's okay for a neighbor who lives two doors away. My father would rather I spent my time on such texts than on Jane Austen or Nabokov?" she added, rather mischievously.

We were not startled by Nassrin's erudite allusions to the works of Ayatollah Khomeini. She was referring to a famous text by Khomeini, the equivalent of his dissertation—required to be written by all who reach the rank of ayatollah—aimed at responding to the questions and dilemmas that could be posed to them by their disciples. Many others before Khomeini had written in almost identical manner. What was disturbing was that these texts were taken seriously by people who ruled us and in whose hands lay our fate and the fate of our country. Every day on national television and radio these guardians of morality and culture would make similar statements and discuss such matters as if they were the most serious themes for contemplation and consideration.

AZAR NAFISI (C.1955–), Iran / United States

T. 1

Frutex Lauri folio pendulo, fructu
tricocco Semine nigro Splendente.
Red Wood.

Psitticus Paradisis.
The Parrot of Paradise

The Passing Wisdom of Birds

ON THE EIGHTH OF NOVEMBER, 1519, Hernando Cortés and four hundred Spanish soldiers marched self-consciously out of the city of Iztapalapa, Mexico, and started across the great Iztapalapan Causeway separating the lakes of Xochimilco and Chalco. They had been received the afternoon before in Iztapalapa as demigods; but they stared now in disbelief at what lay before them. Reflecting brilliantly on the vast plain of dark water like a landscape of sunlit chalk, its lines sharp as cut stone in the dustless air at 7200 feet, was the Aztec Byzantium—Tenochtitlán. Mexico City.

It is impossible to know what was in the facile, highly charged mind of Cortés that morning, anticipating his first meeting with the reluctant Montezuma; but Bernal Díaz, who was present, tells us what was on the minds of the soldiers. They asked each other was it *real*—gleaming Iztapalapa behind them, the smooth causeway beneath their feet, imposing Tenochtitlán ahead? The Spanish had been in the New World for twenty-seven years, but what they discovered in the Valley of Mexico that fall "had never been heard of or seen before, nor even dreamed about" in their world. What astounded them was not, solely, the extent and sophistication of the engineering that divided and encompassed the lakes

Parrot of Paradise, M. Catesby (1679–1749), England

surrounding Tenochtitlán; nor the evidence that a separate culture, utterly different from their own, pursued a complex life in this huge city. It was the depth and pervasiveness of the natural beauty before their senses.

The day before, they had strolled the spotless streets of Iztapalapa through plots of full-blossomed flowers, arranged in patterns and in colors pleasing to the eye; through irrigated fruit orchards; and into still groves of aromatic trees, like cedar. They sat in the shade of bright cotton awnings in quiet stone patios and marveled at the robustness and the well-tended orderliness of the vegetable gardens around them. Roses glowed against the lime-washed walls of the houses like garnets and alexandrites. In the hour before sunset, the cool, fragrant air was filled with the whirr and flutter of birds, and lit with birdsong.

That had been Iztapalapa. Mexico City, they thought, even as their leader dismounted that morning with solemn deliberation from that magical creature, the horse, to meet an advancing Montezuma ornately caparisoned in gold and silver and bird feathers—Mexico City, they thought as they approached, could only outdo Iztapalapa. And it did. With Montezuma's tentative welcome they were free to wander in its various precincts. Mexico City confirmed the image of a people gardening with meticulous care and with exquisite attention to line and detail at the edge of nature.

It is clear from Díaz's historical account that the soldiers were stunned by the physical beauty of Tenochtitlán. Venice came to their minds in comparison, because of its canals; but Venice was not as intensely fresh, as well lit as Mexico City. And there was not to be found in Venice, or in Salamanca or Paris for that matter, anything like the great aviaries where thousands of birds—white egrets, energetic wrens and thrushes, fierce accipiters, brilliantly colored parrots—were housed and tended. They were as captivating, as fabulous, as the displays of flowers: vermilion flycatchers, copper-tailed trogons, green jays, blue-throated hummingbirds, and summer tanagers. Great blue herons, brooding condors.

And throughout the city wild birds nested.

Even Cortés, intensely preoccupied with politics, with guiding a diplomacy of conquest in the region, noticed the birds. He was struck, too, by the affinity of the Mexican people for their gardens and for the measured and intricate flow of water through their city. He took time to write Charles V in Spain, describing it all.

Cortés's men, says Díaz, never seemed to tire of the arboretums, gardens, and aviaries in the months following their entry into the city. By June 1520, however, Cortés's psychological manipulation of Montezuma and a concomitant arrogance, greed, and disrespect on the part of the Spanish military force had become too much for the Mexicans, and they drove them out. Cortés, relentless and vengeful, returned to the Valley of Mexico eleven months later with a larger army and laid siege to the city. Canal by canal, garden by garden, home by home, he destroyed what he had described to Charles V as "the most beautiful city in the world." On June 16, in a move calculated to humiliate and frighten the Mexican people, Cortés set fire to the aviaries.

BARRY LOPEZ (1945–), United States

Plate LXXIV

P.O. del et lith.

R.B & R. imp.

Piaya pluvialis, Linn.

(p. 277)

Beware the Jubjub bird, and shun
The frumious Bandersnatch!

VIII ~

THEN THE BIRDS ATTACKED

Avian defence and flying nightmares

Chestnut-Bellied Cuckoo, P.H. Gosse (1810–1888), England

Because humans often imbue them with their own best and most spiritual qualities, it's disturbing when birds appear in darker, more threatening forms. There is something particularly horrible about the bird-like souls of the dead—the good and the wicked together—that we meet in the Epic of Gilgamesh, crouching enfolded in their dusty wings amidst the gloom of Mesopotamia's wretched afterlife.

While the Biblical God sent plagues such as mice and hemorrhoids[1] in punishment of the wicked, He didn't often send birds. It's true that the bittern and the cormorant, the owl and the raven, possess sites ravaged by the Lord's wrath, but they weren't the instruments of it. Nevertheless, there's a strain in our tradition that holds birds responsible for acts of aggression against us.

Given our own formidable talents for habitat destruction and slaughter, birds have a clear case for revenge, though it doesn't seem to have crossed their minds often except in parables and fiction. However, there are some good stories of deliberate feathered vengeance, one of which was told to me in New South Wales. An exasperated homeowner frightened off two Black Cockatoos that

1. I. Samuel, 5–6.

266

had been repeatedly tearing shingles from the roof of his house. He must have done it in an unpleasant manner, said my informant, because the following day a great mob of Black Cockatoos descended on his house and demolished the entire roof.

Some birds are simply dangerous by nature, especially if hungry or defending territory. Unexpectedly meeting a cassowary in the rainforest of northern Queensland is an interesting experience: staring into its pale blue face beneath a horn-covered helmet, one remembers that these birds, which stand up to 1.8 metres in height, are said to kill more people each year than polar bears do, and that their preferred method is to disembowel a victim with terrible kicks from their powerful, sharp-nailed feet.

Natural avian aggression translates powerfully into myth and story. When a creature traditionally associated with the soul becomes a threat, you know there'll be the devil to pay. Malevolence on wings is irresistible to storytellers, and historically they've taken full advantage of it.

The Greek poet Aeschylus was said to have been killed when an eagle, mistaking his bald head for a rock, dropped a tortoise on it to break the shell. That was simply a bird's mistake. On the other hand, Zeus knew what he was doing when he raped Leda in the guise of a swan, and the eagle that tore at Prometheus's liver was taking orders. The Roc in *The Thousand and One Nights*, the monstrous crow in *Alice Through the Looking Glass*, even Poe's Raven— none have kindly intentions. The stories in this section ring changes on a venerable tradition of scary birds.

G.G.

The Black Beast

Where is the Black beast?
Crow, like an owl, swivelled his head.
Where is the Black Beast?
Crow hid in its bed, to ambush it.
Where is the Black Beast?
Crow sat in its chair, telling loud lies against the Black Beast.
Where is it?
Crow shouted after midnight, pounding the walls with a
    last.
Where is the Black Beast?
Crow split his enemy's skull to the pineal gland.
Where is the Black Beast?
Crow crucified a frog under a microscope, he peered into
    the brain of a dogfish.
Crow killed his brother and turned him inside out to stare
    at his colour.
Where is the Black Beast?
Crow roasted the earth to a clinker, he charged into space—
Where is the Black Beast?
The silences of space decamped, space flitted in every
    direction—
Where is the Black Beast?
Crow flailed immensely through the vacuum, he screeched
    after the disappearing stars—
Where is it? Where is the Black Beast?

TED HUGHES (1930–1998), England

FREAK ACTION OF A CRAZY BIRD

CASPARIS REPORTS that early in his eagle-hunting career in the Big Bend, an enormous eagle crash-dived his plane before he could shoot, tore through the window, ripped off several feet of the fuselage and showered him with shattered glass. This incident may be dismissed as accidental, as the freak action of a crazy bird, as mere panic, or anyway you like. But

Golden Eagle, J.M. Wolf (1820–1899) and H.C. Richter (1821–1902), England

at that, it curiously confirms reports of the reactions of the golden eagle to first appearances of airplanes in the skies of France. The French army authorities, on reports by aviators of eagle encounters, seriously considered training eagles to attack enemy planes, and a French aeronautical journal proclaimed boldly that no airplane could withstand such an avian offensive. The British Air Ministry issued official instructions to airmen on proper tactics to pursue when assailed by eagles. J. Wentworth Day reports a concerted attack by two eagles on a three-motored, all-steel passenger plane near Allahbad. "The first eagle," he says, "flew straight into the middle engine, while the second dived from ten thousand feet, and went through the steel wing like a stone, ripping a great hole."[1] Of course, modern planes have little to fear from eagles or other birds individually, but the encountering by plane of migration flights, especially flights of large birds in considerable number, is said still to offer a considerable hazard.

ROY BEDICHEK (1878–1959), United States
from *Adventures with a Texas Naturalist*

1. *Birds vs. Planes*, by Frank W. Lane, *Natural History,* Vol. LV, No. 4, p. 165, April 1946. Mr. Lane also discusses in this article the reactions of many other birds to the airplane.

CURLEW.

The Night of the Curlews

WE WERE SITTING, the three of us, around the table, when someone put a coin in the slot and the Wurlitzer played once more the record that had been going all night. The rest happened so fast that we didn't have time to think. It happened before we could remember where we were, before we could get back our sense of location. One of us reached his hand out over the counter, groping (we couldn't see the hand, we heard it), bumped into a glass, and then was still, with both hands resting on the hard surface. Then the three of us looked for ourselves in the darkness and found ourselves there, in the joints of the thirty fingers piled up on the counter. One of us said:

"Let's go."

And we stood up as if nothing had happened. We still hadn't had time to get upset.

Curlew, F.O. Morris (1810–1893), Ireland/England

In the hallway, as we passed, we heard the nearby music spinning out at us. We caught the smell of sad women sitting and waiting. We felt the prolonged emptiness of the hall before us while we walked towards the door, before the other smell came out to greet us, the sour smell of the woman sitting by the door. We said:

"We're leaving."

The woman didn't answer anything. We heard the creak of a rocking chair, rising up as she stood. We heard the footsteps on the loose board and the return of the woman again, when the hinges creaked once more and the door closed behind us.

We turned around. Right there, behind us, there was a harsh, cutting breeze of an invisible dawn, and a voice that said:

"Get out of the way, I'm coming through with this."

We moved back. And the voice spoke again:

"You're still against the door."

And, only then, when we'd moved to all sides and had found the voice everywhere, did we say:

"We can't get out of here. The curlews have pecked out our eyes."

Then we heard several doors open. One of us let go of the other hands and we heard him dragging along in the darkness, weaving, bumping into the things that surrounded us. He spoke from somewhere in the darkness.

"We must be close," he said. "There's a smell of piled-up trunks around here."

We felt the contact of his hands again. We leaned against the wall and another voice passed by then, but in the opposite direction.

"They might be coffins," one of us said.

The one who had dragged himself into the corner and was breathing beside us now said:

"They're trunks. Ever since I was little I've been able to tell the smell of stored clothing."

Then we moved in that direction. The ground was soft and smooth, fine earth that had been walked on. Someone held out a hand. We felt the contact with long, live skin, but we no longer felt the wall opposite.

"This is a woman," we said.

The other one, the one who had spoken of trunks, said:

"I think she's asleep."

The body shook under our hands, trembled, we felt it slip away, not as if it had got out of our reach, but as if it had ceased to exist. Still, after an instant in which we remained motionless, stiffened, leaning against each other's shoulders, we heard her voice.

"Who's there?" it said.

"It's us," we replied without moving.

The movement of the bed could be heard, the creaking and the shuffling of feet looking for slippers in the darkness. Then we pictured the seated woman, looking at us as when she still hadn't awakened completely.

"What are you doing here?" she asked.

And we answered:

"We don't know. The curlews pecked out our eyes."

The voice said that she'd heard something about that. That the newspapers had said that three men had been drinking in a courtyard where there were five or six curlews. Seven

OVERLEAF: *Long-Billed Curlew* (detail), J.J. Audubon (1785–1851), France/United States

273

curlews. One of the men began singing like a curlew, imitating them.

"The worst was that he was an hour behind," she said. "That was when the birds jumped on the table and pecked out their eyes."

She said that's what the newspapers had said, but nobody had believed them. We said:

"If people had gone there, they'd have seen the curlews."

And the woman said:

"They did. The courtyard was full of people the next day, but the woman had already taken the curlews somewhere else."

When he turned around, the woman stopped speaking. There was the wall again. By just turning around we would find the wall. Around us, surrounding us, there was always a wall. One let go of our hands again. We heard him crawling again, smelling the ground, saying:

"Now I don't know where the trunks are. I think we're somewhere else now."

And we said:

"Come here. Somebody's here next to us."

We heard him come close. We felt him stand up beside us and again his warm breath hit us in the face.

"Reach out that way," we told him. "There's someone we know there."

He must have reached out, he must have moved towards the place we indicated, because an instant later he came back to tell us:

"I think it's a boy."

And we told him:

"Fine. Ask him if he knows us."

276

He asked the question. We heard the apathetic and simple voice of the boy, who said:

"Yes, I know you. You're the three men whose eyes were pecked out by the curlews."

Then an adult voice spoke. The voice of a woman who seemed to be behind a closed door, saying:

"You're talking to yourself again."

And the child's voice, unconcerned, said:

"No. The men who had their eyes pecked out by the curlews are here again."

There was a sound of hinges and then the adult voice, closer than the first time.

"Take them home," she said.

And the boy said:

"I don't know where they live."

And the adult voice said:

"Don't be mean. Everybody knows where they live ever since the night the curlews pecked their eyes out."

Then she went on in a different tone, as if she were speaking to us:

"What happened is that nobody wanted to believe it and they say it was a fake item made up by the papers to boost their circulation. No one has seen the curlews."

And he said:

"But nobody would believe me if I led them along the street."

We didn't move. We were still, leaning against the wall, listening to her. And the woman said:

"If this one wants to take you it's different. After all, nobody would pay much attention to what a boy says."

The child's voice cut in:

"If I go out on to the street with them and say that they're the men who had their eyes pecked out by the curlews, the boys will throw stones at me. Everybody on the street says it couldn't have happened."

There was a moment of silence. Then the door closed again and the boy spoke:

"Besides, I'm reading *Terry and the Pirates* right now."

Someone said in our ear:

"I'll convince him."

He crawled over to where the voice was.

"I like it," he said. "At least tell us what happened to Terry this week."

He's trying to gain his confidence, we thought. But the boy said:

"That doesn't interest me. The only thing I like are the colours."

"Terry's in a maze," we said.

And the boy said:

"That was Friday. Today's Sunday and what I like are the colours," and he said it with a cold, dispassionate, indifferent voice.

When the other one came back, we said:

"We've been lost for almost three days and we haven't had a moment's rest."

And one said:

"All right. Let's rest awhile, but without letting go of each other's hands."

We sat down. An invisible sun began to warm us on the shoulders. But not even the presence of the sun interested us. We felt it there, everywhere, having already lost the notion of distance, time, direction. Several voices passed.

"The curlews pecked out our eyes," we said.

And one of the voices said:

"These here took the newspapers seriously."

The voices disappeared. And we kept on sitting, like that, shoulder to shoulder, waiting, in that passing of voices, in that passing of images, for a smell or a voice that was known to us to pass. The sun was above our heads, still warming us. Then someone said:

"Let's go towards the wall again."

And the others, motionless, their heads lifted towards the invisible light:

"Not yet. Let's just wait till the sun begins to burn us on the face."

GABRIEL GARCÍA MÁRQUEZ (1925–), Colombia

Incendiary Birds

The use of animals as a delivery system to carry flammable materials occurs elsewhere in the ancient world. Chinese and Arabic military manuals, for example, suggested smearing crows, and other birds with incendiary substances to set fire to enemy tents and Kautiliya's Arthashastra recommended attaching incendiary powders to birds, cats, mongooses and monkeys . . . Kautilya suggested capturing only vultures, crows, and pigeons that nested in the besieged city's walls. . . .

Genghis Khan relied on the same "homing principle on a large scale during his conquest of China in AD 1211. During his siege of several fortified cities, it is said that he offered to lift the siege in exchange for 1,000 cats and 10,000 swallows. "These were duly handed over," writes the historian David Morgan, and the Mongols tied flammable material to the tails of the birds and cats and ignited them. When the creatures were released, they fled home, setting each city on fire, and Genghis Khan easily stormed the burning cities.

Adrienne Mayor (contemporary), United States

Celtic helmet (3rd century BC), Romania

FROM WILSON'S AMERICAN ORNITHOLOGY

MY WORTHY FRIEND MR. GARDINER informs me, that they (the osprey) have even been known to fix their claws in a negro's head, who was attempting to climb to their nest; and I had lately a proof of their daring spirit in this way, through the kindness of a friend, resident, for a few weeks, at Great Egg Harbor. I had requested of him the favor to transmit me, if possible, a live Fish Hawk, for the purpose of making a drawing of it, which commission he very faithfully executed; and I think I cannot better illustrate this part of the bird's character, than by quoting his letter at large:—

> "Beasley's, Great Egg Harbor, 30th June, 1811.
> "Sir,—Mr. Beasley and I went to reconnoitre a Fish Hawk's nest on Thursday afternoon. When I was at the nest, I was struck with so great violence on the crown of the hat, that I thought a hole was made in it. I had ascended fearlessly, and never dreamt of being attacked. I came down quickly. There were in the nest three young ones, about the size of Pullets, which though full feathered, were unable to fly. On Friday morning, I went again to the nest to get a

young one, which I thought I could nurse to a considerable growth, sufficient to answer your purpose, if I should fail to procure an old one, which was represented to me as almost impossible, on account of his shyness, and the danger from his dreadful claws. On taking a young one, I intended to lay a couple of snares in the nest, for which purpose I had a strong cord in my pocket. The old birds were on the tree when Captain H. and I approached it. As a defence, profiting by the experience of yesterday, I took a walking stick with me. When I was about half up the tree, the bird I send you struck at me repeatedly with violence; he flew round, in a small circle, darting at me at every circuit, and I striking at him. Observing that he always described a circle in the air, before he came at me, I kept a *hawk's eye* upon him, and the moment he passed me, I availed myself of the opportunity to ascend. When immediately under the nest, I hesitated at the formidable opposition I met, as his rage appeared to increase with my presumption in invading his premises. But I mounted to the nest. At that moment he darted directly at me with all his force, whizzing through the air, his choler apparently redoubled. Fortunately for me, I struck him on the extreme joint of the right wing with my stick, which brought him to the ground. During this contest, the female was flying round and round at a respectful distance. Captain H. held him till I tied my handkerchief

Osprey, J.M. Wolf (1820–1899) and H.C. Richter (1821–1902), England

about his legs: the captain felt the effect of his claws. I brought away a young one to keep the old one in a good humor. I put them in a very large coop; the young one ate some fish, when broken and put into its throat; but the old one would not eat for two days. He continued sullen and obstinate, hardly changing his position. He walks about now and is approached without danger. He takes very little notice of the young one. A Joseph Smith, working in the field where this nest is, had the curiosity to go up and look at the eggs: the bird clawed his face in a shocking manner; his eye had a narrow escape. I am told that it has never been considered dangerous to approach a Hawk's nest. If this be so, this bird's character is peculiar; his affection for his young, and his valiant opposition to an invasion of his nest, entitle him to conspicuous notice. He is the *prince* of Fish Hawks; his character and his portrait seem worthy of being handed to the historic muse. A Hawk more worthy of the honor which awaits him could not have been found. I hope no accident will happen to him, and that he may fully answer your purpose.—Yours,

"Thomas Smith."

"This morning the female was flying to and fro, making a mournful noise."

ALEXANDER WILSON (1776–1813),
Scotland/United States

DOVE-LOVE

The dove purrs—over and over the dove
purrs its declaration. The wind's tone
changes from tree to tree, the creek on stone
alters its sob and fall, but still the dove
goes insistently on, telling its love
    "I could eat you."

And in captivity, they say, doves do.
Gentle, methodical, starting with the feet
(the ham-pink succulent toes
on their thin stems of rose),
baring feather by feather the wincing meat:
    "I could eat you."

That neat suburban head, that suit of grey,
watchful conventional eye and manicured claw—
these also rhyme with us. The doves play
on one repetitive note that plucks the raw
helpless nerve, their soft "I do. I do.
    I could eat you."

JUDITH WRIGHT (1915–2000), Australia

ALBATROS.

FROM IN PATAGONIA

WE WERE CLOSE TO THE HORN, running with all plain sail set to a spanking breeze on the starboard quarter. It was a Sunday morning. I was walking up and down the main hatch with Chips the Carpenter and he said: 'The girls at home are pulling with both hands.'

It's an old sailor's idea that every ship has a rope with one end made fast to her bows and the other held by the loved ones at home. And when the ship has a fair wind sailors say the girls are pulling hard on the rope. But when the wind is foul, some say there's a knot or a kink in the rope, which won't go through the block; and others say the girls are sparking round with the soldier chaps and have forgotten their sailor laddies.

Just then four bells struck. It was 10 a.m. and my turn to relieve the wheel. I had hardly got the middle spoke to my satisfaction, when the breeze backed northward a couple of points, so that the squaresails took some wind out of the fore-and aft-canvas. The carpenter was still walking up and down when the ship rolled heavily to port. There was no wind in the

Albatros, F. Specht (1839–1909), Germany

main royal staysail and the sheet hung slack in a bight on the deck. The carpenter lost his balance in the roll and, by mistake, laid his foot on the staysail sheet. With the next roll to windward, the sail filled again and tightened the sheet like a fiddle-string and caught Chips between the legs and dropped him in the sea.

I saw him go. I left the wheel a second and threw him a lifebuoy. We put the helm down and threw the ship into the wind, letting the top-gallant and royal halyards fly. While some hands cleared the accident boat, the rest began to get in the kites (as the small sails are called), and in less than ten minutes the boat was on her way to pick up the carpenter, whom we could see swimming strongly.

At the cry 'Man Overboard!' the whole of the 'watch below' had come on deck. First into the accident boat was the apprentice Walter Paton. The Second Mate, Mr Spence, knew Paton couldn't swim much and told him to get out, and Philip Eddy, another apprentice, jumped into his place. Walter was not to be put off, though, and got in over the bows. The boat was in the water before Mr Spence saw him, and I heard a few remarks as they passed under the stern of the ship. Then we lost sight of them in the heavy sea that was running.

The boat left the ship at 10.15, all the crew with their lifebelts on. We were busy for some time getting the ship shortened down. The Captain was aloft on the mizzen crosstrees watching the boat. They had a long pull to windward and it was not till 11.30 that they were close to us coming back. But we couldn't see if they had the carpenter or not.

The Captain gave the order to 'Up Helm' for the purpose of wearing ship, to bring the boat's davits on the lee side and so hoist it aboard, and we all saw Mr Spence stand up and wave his arms. Whether to say they'd got the carpenter, or whether he thought we hadn't seen them, will never be known. But in that one fatal second, his attention was off the boat, and she broached to and capsized. She was close to us, not more than two cables, and we saw them all swimming in the water.

We put the helm down again and brought the ship into the wind. We hurried to get out the second boat, but in a sailing ship this is a very different matter from getting out the first. One boat was always ready, but the others were all bottom up on the skids; and not only bottom up, but stuffed full of gear. The Captain's fowls were in one. All the cabbages for the voyage were in another, and firebuckets and stands were stowed there to prevent them being washed overboard.

The men turned over the port boat first. But just as they had her over, a big wave struck the ship and two of them slipped, and she came down heavily and was staved in the bilge. Meanwhile I was watching the men in the water with glasses. I saw some helping others on to the bottom of the overturned boat. Then I saw Eddy and one of the Able-Seamen leave and swim towards the ship. They swam so close we could see who they were without glasses. But we were drifting faster than they could swim and they had to go back.

After turning over the starboard boat, we had to put a tackle on the main royal backstay to lift it over the side. And I don't know whether the man who put the strop on the backstay was incapable or hurried, but, time after time, the strop slipped and each time the boat came down. And the ship was drifting, drifting to leeward, and we lost sight of the boat and the poor fellows clinging to the keel. But we knew where it was by the flights of birds wheeling round the spot—albatrosses, mollymauks, sooty petrels, stinkpots—all circling round and round.

The second boat, with Mr Flynn in charge, got away, but it was nearly 1 p.m. when she passed under the stern. She had a longer pull to windward and the men were hindered by their lifebelts. And she had a much longer pull back as the ship was drifting to leeward all the time.

We lost sight of her after twenty minutes and there began a weary wait for us, knowing five of our comrades were doing their level best to cling to the upturned keel. The Captain put the ship on one tack and then another, but finally decided to remain hove to and not lose ground. So we lay there straining our eyes for the return of the boat.

At 3.30 we saw her coming back. She came in under the stern but the wind and sea had risen and it was some time before she dared come alongside. By then we had realized the worst and locked the tackles on in silence and hoisted the boat inboard. Two or three of the men were bleeding about the head, those whose caps and sou' westers were not fastened. When the ship was back on course, we were able to ask questions and the gist of what we heard was this:

They had found the boat. They had brought back the lifebuoy I threw to the carpenter, and three of the five lifebelts, and had seen the other two in the sea, but not a sign of anyone. Then the birds attacked and they had to fight them off with stretchers. They swooped on their heads and took their caps off, and the men who were bleeding were struck by the cruel beaks of the albatrosses. When they examined the lifebelts and found all the strings untied, they knew what had happened. The birds had gone for the men in the water and gone for their eyes. And the poor chaps had willingly untied the strings and sunk when they saw that no help came, for they couldn't fight the birds with any hope of winning. The lifebuoy proved they had rescued the carpenter before the second accident occurred. It made us all the sadder to know that they had accomplished this mission.

After six and a half hours they relieved me from the wheel. It was the longest trick I ever experienced. I went down to the half-deck to get something to eat, but when I saw Walter's and Philip's bedclothes turned down and their pants lying on their chests, and their boots on the floor, just as they had left them at the cry 'Man Overboard!', I lost control of myself, thought no more of being hungry and could do nothing but sob. Later the Skipper told the Third Mate to take me away and let me sleep in his cabin.

'It's enough to drive the boy mad, in there with all those empty bunks.'

BRUCE CHATWIN (1940–1989), England

THE VULTURE

A VULTURE WAS HACKING AT MY FEET. It had already torn my boots and stockings to shreds, now it was hacking at the feet themselves. Again and again it struck at them, then circled several times restlessly round me, then returned to continue its work. A gentleman passed by, looked on for a while, then asked me why I suffered the vulture. "I'm helpless," I said. "When it came and began to attack me, I of course tried to drive it away, even to strangle it, but these animals are very strong, it was about to spring at my face, but I preferred to sacrifice my feet. Now they are almost torn to bits." "Fancy letting yourself be tortured like this!" said the gentleman. "One shot and that's the end of the vulture." "Really?" I said. "With pleasure," said the gentleman, "I've only got to go home and get my gun. Could you wait another half hour?" "I'm not sure about that," said I, and stood for a moment rigid with pain. Then I said: "Do try it in any case, please." "Very well," said the gentleman, "I'll be as quick as I can." During this conversation the vulture had been calmly listening, letting its eye rove between me and the gentleman. Now I realized that it had understood everything; it took wing, leaned far back to gain impetus, and then, like a javelin thrower, thrust its beak through my mouth, deep into me. Falling back, I was relieved to feel him drowning irretrievably in my blood, which was filling every depth, flooding every shore.

FRANZ KAFKA (1883–1924), Czech

Griffon Vulture, F.O. Morris (1810–1893), Ireland / England

from The Head-Hunters of Borneo

The Sultan's leisure time is pretty equally divided between the hareem and the cock-pit. He boasts of having forty-two wives, i.e. four privileged wives and thirty-eight concubines, the latter of whom he can remove at his pleasure. The number of children born to him averages just two to each wife and concubine, or eighty-four altogether, most of whom are still alive. These children are a practical commentary on an observation which the Sultan once made to me when speaking of the politics of his country,—

"Me want Koetei make big country; want plenty people."

Like Santa Anna, the wretched Mexican President, and like nearly every Malay that ever breathed, he takes the greatest delight in cock-fighting. Not a day passes but some important contest takes place on his premises. The crowd, with their cocks, generally begin to assemble between two and three in the afternoon, and his Highness is soon on the spot closely examining the birds that are going to fight, the owners of which bring them to him, grovelling at full length on the ground. The Sultan puts the spurs—curved steel blades, three inches long, and as sharp as a razor—on his own birds, rubs the blade with lemon, in order that any wound inflicted by the combatants may smart the more, and does not scruple to show his confidence in his birds by betting on them to any extent. Birds pitted against each other under such conditions are very soon *hors de combat*. As soon as one of the combatants is declared to be defeated, the executioner—a functionary as necessary to a properly conducted cock-pit as a

Asaf-al-Daula (Nawab of Oudh), artist unknown (c.1830–1835)

time-keeper to a prize-fight—decapitates it with his mandau, first, however, allowing the conqueror to give it a final coup by biting it with its beak on the neck or head.

The Sultan has over sixty large fighting cocks, each of which is kept in a room in the Palace under an oval wicker cage, somewhat resembling a lobster-pot with the bottom taken out. Every day these birds, or such of them as survive the daily contests, are taken to the river to be washed, being afterwards fed on maize and rice.

The loud and pertinacious crowing of the cocks in almost every village in Borneo, Java, Sumatra, or indeed any of the islands of the Indian Archipelago, is an experience not likely to be forgotten by any European traveller there. Before sunrise every day one restless bird utters his long drawn out clarion cry of challenge, which is taken up by dozens, by scores, by hundreds of birds throughout the village, who then continue the crowing exercise, in detachments, volley firing as it were, or singing in a discordant chorus, till such time as the whole village is awake. As soon as the inhabitants begin to move about these very undesirable neighbours seem satisfied with the result of their performance, and are silent. The effect of sleeping in close contiguity to a select company of sixty of the finest, strongest, heartiest, and gamest of the game cocks of Koetei may be imagined. I have many a day suffered severe headache as a result of the combined inharmonious battle-cries of these birds.

CARL BOCK (1849–1932), Norway/Denmark/England

Le Désespoir de la chimère, A. Séon (1855–1917), France

The Avenging Parrot

THE CHARPILLON, who was well known in London, and I believe is still alive, was one of those beauties in whom it is difficult to find any positive fault. Her hair was chestnut coloured, and astonishingly long and thick, her blue eyes were at once languorous and brilliant, her skin, faintly tinged with a rosy hue, was of a dazzling whiteness; she was tall for her age, and seemed likely to become as tall as Pauline. Her breast was perhaps a little small, but perfectly shaped, her hands were white and plump, her feet small, and her gait had something noble and gracious. Her features were of that exquisite sensibility which gives so much charm to the fair sex, but nature had given her a beautiful body and a deformed soul. This siren had formed a design to wreck my happiness even before she knew me, and as if to add to her triumph she told me as much.

. . . "I once took a violent fancy for the little hussy," said (Pembroke). "It was one evening when I was at Vauxhall, and I offered her twenty guineas if she would come and take a little walk with me in a dark alley. She said she would come if I gave her the money in advance, which I was fool enough to do. She went with me, but as soon as we were alone she ran away, and I could not catch her again, though I looked for her all the evening."

"You ought to have boxed her ears before everybody."

"I should have got into trouble, and people would have laughed at me besides. I preferred to despise her and the money too. Are you in love with her?"

"No; but I am curious, as you were."

"Take care! she will do all in her power to entrap you."

(After subjecting Casanova to a series of humiliating, and predictably expensive frustrations, La Charpillon charges him with assault. A blind judge throws the charges out. Although the failed lover goes free, he is not a happy man.)

A FEW DAYS AFTERWARDS, as I was walking idly about, I passed a place called the Parrot Market. As I was amusing myself by looking at these curious birds, I saw a fine young one in a cage, and asked what language it spoke. They told me that it was quite young and did not speak at all yet, so I bought it for ten guineas. I thought I would teach the bird a pretty speech, so I had the cage hung by my bed, and repeated dozens of times every day the following sentence: "The Charpillon is a bigger whore than her mother."

The only end I had in view was my private amusement, and in a fortnight the bird had learnt the phrase with the utmost exactness; and every time it uttered the words it accompanied them with a shriek of laughter which I had not taught it, but which made me laugh myself.

One day Gondar heard the bird, and told me that if I sent it to the Exchange I should certainly get fifty guineas for it. I welcomed the idea, and resolved to make the parrot the instrument of my vengeance against the woman who had treated me so badly. I secured myself from fear of the law, which is severe in such cases, by entrusting the bird to my negro, to whom such merchandise was very suitable.

For the first two or three days my parrot did not attract much attention, its observations being in French; but as soon as those who knew the subject of them had heard it, its audience increased and bids were made. Fifty guineas seemed rather too much, and my negro wanted me to lower the price, but I would not agree, having fallen in love with this odd revenge.

In the course of a week Goudar came to inform me of the effect the parrot's criticism had produced in the Charpillon family. As the vendor was my negro, there could be no doubt as to whom it belonged, and who had been its master of languages. Goudar said that the Charpillon thought my vengeance very ingenious, but that the mother and aunts were furious. They had consulted several counsel, who agreed in saying that a parrot could not be indicted for libel, but that they could make me pay dearly for my jest if they could prove that I had been the bird's instructor. Goudar warned me to be careful of owning to the fact, as two witnesses would suffice to undo me.

The facility with which false witnesses may be produced in London is something dreadful. I have myself seen the word evidence written in large characters in a window; this is as much as to say that false witnesses may be procured within.

The St. James's Chronicle contained an article on my parrot, in which the writer remarked that the ladies whom the bird insulted must be very poor and friendless, or they would have bought it at once, and have thus prevented the thing from becoming the talk of the town. He added,—

"The teacher of the parrot has no doubt made the bird an instrument of his vengeance, and has displayed his wit in doing so; he ought to be an Englishman."

I met my good friend Edgar, and asked him why he had not bought the little slanderer.

"Because it delights all who know anything about the object of the slander," said he.

At last Jarbe found a purchaser for fifty guineas, and I heard afterwards that Lord Grosvenor had bought it to please the Charpillon, with whom he occasionally diverted himself.

Thus my relations with that girl came to an end. I have seen her since with the greatest indifference, and without any renewal of the old pain.

Jacques Casanova de Seingalt (1725–1798), Italy / France

839.

Brown Pelican
(Pelecanus occidentalis).

Mark Catesby 1725
Vol. 15
23

June 20 {1850} The note of the whip-poor-will,
borne over the fields is the voice with which
the woods and moonlight woo me.
HENRY DAVID THOREAU

Hope is a waking dream.
ARISTOTLE

IX ~

SOME BLESSED HOPE

Birds and the nostalgic human soul

Brown Pelican, C. Collins (c.1680–1744), England

A GREAT MANY BIRDWATCHERS—from those who simply maintain feeders in their gardens to those, more obsessed, who wander the world in search of new and better birds—have stumbled onto a seductive truth: paying attention to birds, being mindful of them, is being mindful of Life itself. We seldom think of it this clearly, but sometimes, unexpectedly, we are overtaken by a sense of wonder and gratitude. Surely it is the encounter with a force much larger than ourselves that moves us.

Recently I was in the Canadian Arctic. We'd put ashore on the south coast of Hudson Strait and were walking in an expansively beautiful river valley when one of our party spotted a white phase gyrfalcon perched on a boulder high on the opposite hill. These are wonderful birds, fiercely majestic and much coveted by wealthy falconers. As we watched, it launched itself, dashing low over the ancient rocks in pursuit of a passing raven—whereupon the chase was on. Desperately twisting and turning, the raven seemed at each instant about to be caught. Then another raven appeared. This second one was clearly striving to position itself so it could help its companion should the gyrfalcon manage to seize it. As the pursuit went on, with the white bird hard on the black bird's tail, I sensed something akin to the notion of fateful inevitability that drives classical tragedy. Raven, the Trickster and wolf-bird, is one of my favourite birds and yet the gyrfalcon is equally wondrous; furthermore, it needed to eat the Raven in order to survive. That's the way things often are.

But not this time. The white bird eventually gave up and returned to preen on its boulder, and the ravens settled to ground halfway down the hill. Then I noticed a third raven circling effortlessly above the valley. Our guide said it had been there all along. Perhaps the gyrfalcon had decided it wouldn't be wise to take on three ravens at once. The chase may even have turned into a joyful form of serious play.

At its best, in its heightened moments, birdwatching can encourage a state of being close to rapture—the forgetfulness that blends the individual consciousness with something other than itself. Some people call it "flow," others "enlightenment."

We can't predict these moments, nor can we fully recapture them, because—in some odd way—they have no content. It's only afterwards, when the self returns—with all its familiar baggage— that we recognize the fact that something utterly liberating has occurred.

The excerpts in this section explore emotionally significant and even hopeful avian encounters. But like most important things in our lives, Hope—whether Blessed or otherwise—must be taken on faith.

Hardy's Darkling Thrush is an aged bird, "frail, gaunt, and small," that nevertheless sings ecstatically. The poet can't for the life of him see what's prompted the creature to "fling his soul / Upon the growing gloom." All he can conclude is that the bird knows something he doesn't. Despite its decrepit condition, its song is charged with the passionate energy of life; and that, after all, is at the heart of everything, including Hope itself.

Some will say that this is a highly Romantic notion, especially in our age. And so it is. And I find it exhilarating.

G. G.

305

FROM BURNT NORTON

I

Time present and time past
Are both perhaps present in time future
And time future contained in time past.
If all time is eternally present
All time is unredeemable.
What might have been is an abstraction
Remaining a perpetual possibility
Only in a world of speculation.
What might have been and what has been
Point to one end, which is always present.
Footfalls echo in the memory
Down the passage which we did not take
Towards the door we never opened
Into the rose-garden. My words echo
Thus, in your mind.
                    But to what purpose
Disturbing the dust on a bowl of rose-leaves
I do not know.

Other echoes
Inhabit the garden. Shall we follow?
Quick, said the bird, find them, find them,
Round the corner. Through the first gate,
Into our first world, shall we follow
The deception of the thrush? Into our first world.
There they were, dignified, invisible,
Moving without pressure, over the dead leaves,
In the autumn heat, through the vibrant air,
And the bird called, in response to
The unheard music hidden in the shrubbery,
And the unseen eyebeam crossed, for the roses
Had the look of flowers that are looked at.
There they were as our guests, accepted and accepting.
So we moved, and they, in a formal pattern,
Along the empty alley, into the box circle,
To look down into the drained pool.
Dry the pool, dry concrete, brown edged,
And the pool was filled with water out of sunlight,
And the lotos rose, quietly, quietly,
The surface glittered out of heart of light,
And they were behind us, reflected in the pool.
Then a cloud passed, and the pool was empty.
Go, said the bird, for the leaves were full of children,
Hidden excitedly, containing laughter.
Go, go, go, said the bird: human kind
Cannot bear very much reality.
Time past and time future
What might have been and what has been
Point to one end, which is always present.

T.S. ELIOT (1888–1965), United States/England

Californian Partridge, J.J. Audubon (1785–1851),
France / United States

WILD SWANS

I looked in my heart while the wild swans went over.
And what did I see I had not seen before?
Only a question less or a question more;
Nothing to match the flight of wild birds flying.
Tiresome heart, forever living and dying,
House without air, I leave you and lock your door.
Wild swans, come over the town, come over
The town again, trailing your legs and crying!

EDNA ST. VINCENT MILLAY (1892–1950), United States

Two Swans, O. Eckmann (1865–1902), Germany

The Pigeon and the Parakeet

HER SORROW WAS GREAT, but a child's night is vaster still. One morning she emerged. She was smiling. When she realized what had happened she was angry and reproached herself for her inconstancy. But do or say what she would, her sorrow continued to fade. She had to resign herself to being not entirely unhappy. Her name was Marie. After her father's death they had put her in a convent. Black suited her. She was blonde and a dreamer. All about her, her companions played, laughing and shouting. She felt the giddy motion of their round, but was afraid to join in and remained to one side, a blue parakeet on her left shoulder. This bird had replaced her heart. It prevented her from giving in to her age and to the pleasures of the moment. It kept her in a kind of semi-happiness, a semi-sadness.

The nuns were full of concern for this unusual child, grieved by her reserve, which at the same time endeared her to them, and they longed to see her happiness complete. One day one of them seized the parakeet, threw it outside and shut the window. "Aha!" said this nun, "now you'll be like all the rest." Marie would have liked nothing better, but the bird had other ideas. Once outside, it began flying at the window, beating its wings and beak against the panes, frantically, cease-lessly, until in the end the whole class was distracted. So, in the general interest, it was decided that Marie should be allowed her little peculiarity. She did not learn very much, but she disturbed no one. And the nuns loved her as if she had been their own daughter. When she had grown up they tried to keep her with them. They asked very little, and then it was for the Lord: in return for food, shelter and salvation, the sacrifice of her hair. Marie accepted. They brought scissors and a cage.

"Why the cage?"

"To shut the bird in."

"Aie!" cried Marie.

The parakeet was digging its claws into her shoulder. Its disapproval brought the ceremony to an end. Marie set out to discover the world. The convent was in the middle of a forest. She entered it, the parakeet trembling on her shoulder. It was the kind of rare and beautiful day that comes only once in a lifetime. The happy girl walked on until the sun went down before her, radiant portal of the night.

Now the hunter was also in the forest. He had killed nothing, and he was angry. Suddenly, through the branches and the green mist, he caught sight of a blue bird. He took aim, fired and ran. . . . To his great surprise he found, beside the dead bird, an unconscious girl! He took her in his arms and carried her off.

When Marie awoke next morning there was a young man beside her, who, in a few words, filled her in on what had happened. Oh! how gallant he was! Marie, ashamed that he had gone to so much trouble, apologized and tried to find words to thank him. The hunter did the same. They were embarrassed and very moved.

Rock Dove, F.O. Morris (1810–1893), Ireland/England

"Farewell," the girl said at last.

"Wait!"

The hunter was holding a pigeon.

"Take it," he said.

Marie put her hand to her shoulder.

"My parakeet!"

And she burst into tears. In his few words the hunter had not told all. He admitted the rest: the blue parakeet was dead; he had killed it; he was desperately sorry. To make amends he was offering her his pigeon.

"Take it, please."

The girl looked at the bird through her tears.

"How ugly it is!" she cried.

"It's all I've got."

The hunter looked so crestfallen she felt sorry for him. She took the pigeon and went. The day was different now. A new forest opened up before her. The path gradually widened. She came to the edge of a field. She saw a house and heard a baby cry. She felt drawn to all this. But she was unable to go on; the pigeon had flown off. She ran after it; it brought her back to her starting point. The hunter was waiting.

"You're wicked and a liar," she told him, "I hate you."

Wicked he was, that he owned, but a liar—it was the first he'd heard of it.

"Whose pigeon is this?" she asked.

"Yours. I gave it to you."

"Liar! You didn't give it to me. The proof is that it's come back to you."

Night was falling. Marie and the hunter were reconciled. The next morning the girl set out again, with the pigeon on her shoulder. The hunter was whistling with satisfaction. He was sure she would be back. But soon the day grew long. . . . The pigeon returned alone. Marie had not followed it. The young man's heart sank. He imagined monsters in the night and the girl at their mercy. He set out to look for her. "Marie! Marie!" he called. There was no answer. Suddenly he saw her sitting at the foot of a tree.

"Why didn't you answer me?"

"You don't love me."

"I adore you."

"I've lost everything. You're still free."

"That's true," said the hunter.

He stood up, took aim and shot the pigeon, which was fluttering above his head.

"I may have given you nothing," he went on, "but at least I've kept nothing myself."

The young woman held out her arms to him. A storm broke. They were shivering and unhappy. They emerged from the forest like our first ancestors. The world began anew. God took pity on them. They had a great many children, and the birds came back again.

Jacques Ferron (1921–1985), Canada

imago aquilae

OF THE COUNCIL HE HELD WITH HIS CHIEF MEN ABOUT EMBRACING THE FAITH OF CHRIST, AND HOW THE HIGH PRIEST PROFANED HIS OWN ALTARS.

[AD 627]

THE KING, hearing these words, answered, that he was both willing and bound to receive the faith which he taught; but that he would confer about it with his principal friends and counsellers, to the end that if they also were of his opinion, they might all together be cleansed in Christ the Fountain of Life. Paulinus consenting, the king did as he said; for, holding a council with the wise men, he asked of every one in particular what he thought of the new doctrine, and the new worship that was preached? To which the chief of his own priests, Coifi, immediately answered, "O king, consider what this is which is now preached to us; for I verily declare to you, that the religion which we have hitherto professed has, as far as I can learn, no virtue in it. For none of your people has applied himself more diligently to the worship of our gods than I; and yet there are many who receive greater favours from you, and are more preferred than I, and are more prosperous in all their undertakings. Now if the gods were good for any thing, they would rather forward me, who have been more careful to

Eagle of St. John, Northumbrian Gospel Book (early 8th century), England

317

serve them. It remains, therefore, that if upon examination you find those new doctrines, which are now preached to us, better and more efficacious, we immediately receive them without any delay."

Another of the king's chief men, approving of his words and exhortations, presently added: "The present life of man, O king, seems to me, in comparison of that time which is unknown to us, like to the swift flight of a sparrow through the room wherein you sit at supper in winter, with your commanders and ministers, and a good fire in the midst, whilst the storms of rain and snow prevail abroad; the sparrow, I say, flying in at one door, and immediately out at another, whilst he is within, is safe from the wintry storm; but after a short space of fair weather, he immediately vanishes out of your sight, into the dark winter from which he had emerged. So this life of man appears for a short space, but of what went before, or what is to follow, we are utterly ignorant. If, therefore, this new doctrine contains something more certain, it seems justly to deserve to be followed." The other elders and king's councillors, by Divine inspiration, spoke to the same effect. . . .

THE VENERABLE BEDE (673–735), England

Sioux buffalo horn ceremonial spoon (c.1850), artist unknown

THE DARKLING THRUSH

I leant upon a coppice gate
  When Frost was spectre-gray,
And Winter's dregs made desolate
  The weakening eye of day.
The tangled bine-stems scored the sky
  Like strings from broken lyres,
And all mankind that haunted nigh
  Had sought their household fires.

The land's sharp features seemed to be
    The Century's corpse outleant,
His crypt the cloudy canopy,
    The wind his death-lament.
The ancient pulse of germ and birth
    Was shrunken hard and dry,
And every spirit upon earth
    Seemed fervourless as I.

At once a voice outburst among
    The bleak twigs overhead
In a full-hearted evensong
    Of joy illimited;
An aged thrush, frail, gaunt, and small,
    In blast-beruffled plume,
Had chosen thus to fling his soul
    Upon the growing gloom.

So little cause for carollings
    Of such ecstatic sound
Was written on terrestrial things
    Afar or nigh around,
That I could think there trembled through
    His happy good-night air
Some blessed Hope, whereof he knew
    And I was unaware.

THOMAS HARDY (1840–1928), England

Hermit Thrush, R. Havell (1793–1878), United States

Eagle, Peterborough Bestiary MS53 (early 14th century)

THE EAGLE

AN EAGLE IS CALLED "aquila", from the sharpness ("acumine") of its eyes. Its sight is said to be such that when it is borne by its feathers motionless above the sea, out of view to humans, it can from such height even see the little fish swimming, and descending like a catapult it snatches its prey and carries it ashore. It is a fact that when it grows old its wings become heavy and its eyes are clouded over with a mist, and then it looks for a spring and soars up above it into the heavens, right to the edge of the sun, and there it singes its wings and in the same way burns off the mist from its eyes in the rays of the sun, and then at last hurtling down into the spring it submerges itself three times and is immediately restored with great strength to wings and clarity of sight. *Spiritualiter:* You too, mankind, are like this, for your clothes are old and the eyes of your heart are clouding over; seek out God, the spiritual spring, and lift the eyes of your mind to God, who is the fount of justice, and then your youth will be renewed like an eagle's. It is claimed too that the eagle exposes its chicks to the rays of the sun, holding them in its claw in mid-air. If one of them steadily retains the bold gaze of its eyes, actively keeping watch in the glare of the sunlight, [fol. 199r] then that one is deemed to have vindicated its true nature. However, any which turns away its eyes from the rays of the sun is rejected as being degenerate and unworthy of such a father; and nor is it considered worthy of rearing if it proved unworthy when it was held up. It does not condemn the chick from a cruel nature but from an impartial judgement; and nor does it disown it like one of its own but as if it were rejecting a stranger. . . .

PETERBOROUGH BESTIARY

TENANCIES

This is pain's landscape.
A savage agriculture is practiced
Here; every farm has its
Grandfather or grandmother, gnarled hands
On the cheque-book, a long slow
Pull on the placenta about the neck.
Old lips monopolise the talk
When a friend calls. The children listen
From the kitchen; the children march
With angry patience against the dawn.
They are waiting for someone to die
Whose name is as bitter as the soil
They handle. In clear pools
In the furrows they watch themselves grow old
To the terrible accompaniment of the song
Of the blackbird, that promises them love.

R.S. THOMAS (1913–2000), Wales

FROM KAPUTT

"I wish I could live as Axel Munthe does in Capri," said Prince Eugene. "He seems to live surrounded by flowers and birds, and I sometimes wonder," he added smiling, "whether he truly loves flowers and birds."

"The flowers love him," I said.

"And do the birds love him?"

"They mistake him for an old withered tree."

Prince Eugene was smiling, his eyes half closed. As in previous years, Axel Munthe had spent the summer at Drottningholm Castle, as the King's guest, and he had started back for Italy a few days earlier. I was sorry not to have met him in Stockholm. Five or six months before, on the eve of my departure for Finland, at Capri, I had gone up to the Torre di Materita to take leave of Munthe, who was to give me letters to Sven Hedin, Ernst Manker and other friends of his in Stockholm. Axel Munthe was waiting for me under the pines and cypresses of Materita. He stood there stiff, wooden, sulky; an old green cloak over his shoulders, a little hat perched crossways on his ruffled hair, his lively mischievous eyes hidden behind dark glasses, which gave him something of that mysterious and menacing air that belongs to the blind. Munthe held a police dog on a leash, and although the dog looked tame, as soon as Munthe saw me among the trees, he began to shout to me not to come too close. "Keep away! Keep away!" he shouted, wildly gesticulating with one arm, urging the dog not to leap at me, not to tear my flesh, pretending that he was restraining it with great difficulty, that he

Pelican, T. Jasper (19th century), United States

was scarcely able to hold back the furious thrusts of that wild beast of his that watched my approach quietly wagging its tail in a friendly welcome. I advanced slowly, simulating fear, happy to lend myself to that innocent comedy.

When Axel Munthe is in a good mood, he amuses himself with improvising mischievous jokes at the expense of his friends. And that was perhaps his first good day after some months of raging loneliness. He had gone through a dismal autumn, a prey to his black whims, his irritable melancholy, shut up day after day in his tower, stripped bare and like an old bone gnawed by the sharp teeth of the southwest wind that blows from Ischia, and by the north wind that carries the acrid smell of the Vesuvian sulphur as far as Capri; locked up in his prison damp with brine, amid his faked old pictures, his faked Hellenic marbles, his fifteenth-century Madonnas carved from pieces of Louis XV furniture.

Axel Munthe looked calm that day; after a while, he began talking of the birds of Capri. Every evening toward sunset he comes out of his tower and moves with slow and cautious steps through the park to a spot where the trees thin out and expose the grass to the sky; he stops and waits—stiff, lean, wooden, like an old tree trunk, worn and withered by the sun, by the frost and the storms and with a happy smile hidden amid the hair of his small beard like that of an aged faun; and the birds fly to him in flocks, twittering lovingly; they perch on his shoulders, on his arms, on his hat. They peck at his nose, his lips and his ears. And Munthe remains there, stiff, motionless, talking to his little friends in the sweet Capri dialect, until the sun sets and dives into the blue-green sea; and the birds fly away to their nests all together with a high chirrup of farewell. . . .

"Ah, that rascal Munthe," said Prince Eugene; his voice was loving, trembling a little.

. . . We walked for a while in the park, beneath the pines swollen with wind. Later, Axel Munthe took me to the top-most room of his tower. It must once have been a granary; he uses it now as his bedroom for the black days of loneliness when he shuts himself up as in a prison cell, stopping his ears with cotton in order not to hear a human voice. He sat down on a stool, with a heavy stick between his knees and the dog's leash coiled around his wrist. The dog, crouching at his feet, gazed at me with a frank, sad look. Axel Munthe raised his face; a sudden shadow had overcast his brow. He told me that he could not sleep—that war had killed his sleep; he spent his nights in tortured wakefulness, listening to the call of the wind through the trees, to the distant voice of the sea.

"I hope," he said, "that you have not come to talk about the war."

"I shall not talk to you about the war," I replied.

"Thank you," said Munthe. And suddenly he asked me whether it was true that the Germans were so dreadfully cruel.

"Their cruelty," I replied, "is made of fear; they are ill with fear. They are a sick nation, a *Krankesvolk*."

"Yes, a sick people," said Munthe, tapping the floor with the tip of his cane, and after a long silence he asked me whether it was true that the Germans were thirsting for blood and destruction.

"They are afraid," I replied, "they are afraid of every-thing and everybody; they kill and destroy out of fear. Not that they fear death; no German, man or woman, young or old, fears death. They are not even afraid of suffering. In a way one may say that they like pain. But they are afraid of all that is living, of all that is living outside of themselves and of all that is different from them. The disease from which they suffer is mysterious. They are afraid above all of the weak, of the defenseless, of the sick, of women and of children. They are afraid of the aged. Their fear has always aroused a profound pity in me. If Europe were to feel sorry for them, perhaps the Germans would be healed of their horrible disease."

"They are bloodthirsty then, it is true then, that they butcher people without mercy?" broke in Munthe tapping his stick impatiently on the floor.

"Yes, it is true," I replied. "They kill the defenseless; they hang Jews on the trees in the village squares, burn them alive in their houses, like rats. They shoot peasants and workers in the yards of the *kolkhoz*—the collective farms—and factories. I have seen them laughing, eating and sleeping in the shade of corpses swinging from the branches of trees."

"It is a *Krankesvolk*," said Munthe removing his dark glasses and wiping the lenses carefully with his handkerchief. He had lowered his eyelids. I could not see his eyes. Later he asked me whether it was true that the Germans kill birds.

"No, it is not true," I replied. "They have no time to bother with birds. They have just time enough to bother with human beings. They butcher Jews, workers, peasants. They set fire to towns and villages with savage fury, but they do not kill birds. Oh, how many beautiful birds there are in Russia! Even more beautiful perhaps than those of Capri."

"More beautiful than those of Capri?" asked Axel Munthe in an irritable voice.

"More beautiful and happier," I replied. "There are countless families of the most beautiful birds in the Ukraine.

They fly about in thousands, twittering among the acacia leaves. They rest on the silvery branches of birches, on the ears of wheat, on the golden petals of sunflowers in order to peck the seeds out of the large black centers. They can be heard singing ceaselessly through the rumble of guns, the rattling of machine guns, through the deep hum of aircraft over in the vast Ukrainian plain. They rest on the shoulders of men, on saddles, on the manes of horses, on gun carriages, on rifle barrels, on the Panzers' conning towers, on the boots of the dead. They are not afraid of the dead. They are small, alert, merry birds, some gray, others green; still others red and some yellow. Some are only red or blue on their chests, some only on their necks, some on their tails. Some are white with a blue throat; and I have seen some that are very tiny and proud, all white, spotlessly white. At dawn they begin to sing sweetly in the cornfield, and the Germans raise their heads from a gloomy slumber to listen to their happy song. They fly in thousands over the battlefields on the Dniester, the Dnieper, the Don. They twitter away free and merry, and they are not afraid of the war. They are not afraid of Hitler, of the SS, or of the Gestapo. They do not linger on branches to look down on the slaughter, but they float in the blue singing. They follow from above the armies marching across the limitless plain. The birds of the Ukraine are truly beautiful."

Axel Munthe raised his face, removed his dark glasses, looked at me with his lively, mischievous eyes and smiled. "At least the Germans do not kill birds," he said. "I am really happy that they do not kill birds."

CURZIO MALAPARTE (1898–1957), Italy

To Stephen Spender

25 April, 1936

My colleague O'Neil writes excellent letters from Germany: he says that in Heidelberg the professor of English, lecturing in post-war English literature, has selected, to lecture on, J. B. Priestly, Mary Webb, & Sir Philip Gibbs. Also that he went to a law Court where a man was condemned to 4 months for throwing a stone at a bird—against Goering's new Reichsjagdgesetzbuch[1]—because that is bestial cruelty and the National Socialist Regime is opposed to cruelty in every shape & form.

Isaiah Berlin (1907–1997), Latvia/Russia/England

1. Reich Hunting Code

ABOVE: Pictish birdmen with head between their bills, design on the Cross of Papil, E.A. Armstrong (after Allen 1887)
OPPOSITE: *Scarlet Tanager* (detail), J.J. Audubon (1785–1851), France/United States

THE JACK DAW

There is a bird who by his coat,
And by the hoarseness of his note,
    Might be suppos'd a crow;
A great frequenter of the church,
Where bishop-like he finds a perch,
    And dormitory too.

Above the steeple shines a plate,
That turns and turns, to indicate
    From what point blows the weather;
Look up—your brains begin to swim,
'Tis in the clouds—that pleases him,
    He chooses it the rather.

Fond of the speculative height,
Thither he wings his airy flight,
    And thence securely sees
The bustle and the raree-show
That occupy mankind below,
    Secure and at his ease.

Jackdaw, F.O. Morris (1810–1893), Ireland / England

You think no doubt he sits and muses
On future broken bones and bruises,
    If he should chance to fall;
No not a single thought like that
Employs his philosophic pate,
    Or troubles it at all.

He sees that this great roundabout
The world, with all its motley rout,
    Church, army, physic, law,
Its customs and its businesses
Are no concern at all of his,
    And says, what says he? Caw.

Thrice happy bird! I too have seen
Much of the vanities of men,
    And sick of having seen 'em,
Would chearfully these limbs resign
For such a pair of wings as thine,
    And such a head between 'em.

WILLIAM COWPER (1731–1800), England

Returning, We Hear the Larks

Sombre the night is,
And though we have our lives, we know
What sinister threat lurks there.

Dragging these anguished limbs, we only know
This poison-blasted track opens on our camp—
On a little safe sleep.

But hark! joy—joy—strange joy.
Lo! heights of night ringing with unseen larks.
Music showering our upturned list'ning faces.

Death could drop from the dark
As easily as song—
But song only dropped,
Like a blind man's dreams on the sand
By dangerous tides,
Like a girl's dark hair for she dreams no ruin lies there,
Or her kisses where a serpent hides.

ISAAC ROSENBERG (1890–1918), England

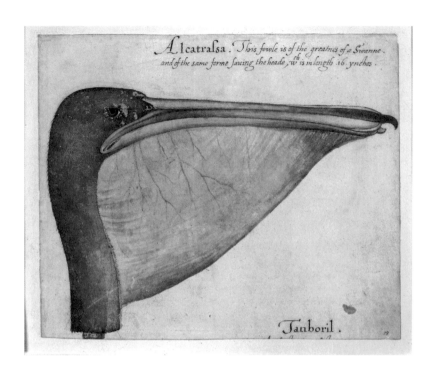

JUDGEMENT

MOSES ROSE FROM HIS SEAT, gigantic and fierce, his Ten
Commandments in his sinewy hands and flashes of lightning
in his eyes.

"How angry he looks," I whispered awestruck to the
patron saint of the dogs.

"He is always angry," the little saint whispered back in
terror.

"Let no more be said about this spirit," thundered
Moses. "The voice I have heard is a voice from the smoking
lips of Satan. Man or demon, away from here! Jehovah, God

Head of a Brown Pelican, J. White (C.1545–1593), England/United States

338

of Israel, put forth Thy hand to smite him down! Burn his flesh and dry up the blood in his veins! Break all his bones! Cut him off from Heaven and earth and send him back to the Hell from whence he came!"

"To Hell! To Hell!" echoed through the Hall of Judgement.

I tried to speak but no sound came from my lips. My heart froze, I felt abandoned by God and man.

"I will look after the dog if it comes to the worst," whispered the little saint at my side.

Suddenly through the awful silence I thought I heard the twitter of birds. A little garden warbler alighted fearlessly on my shoulder and sang in my ear:

"You saved the life of my grandmother, my aunt and my three brothers and sisters from torture and death by the hand of man on that rocky island. Welcome! Welcome!"

At the same moment a skylark picked at my finger and twittered to me:

"I met a flycatcher in Lapland who told me that when you were a boy you mended the wing of one of his ancestors and warmed his frozen body near your heart, and as you opened your hand to set him free you kissed him and said: 'Godspeed little brother! Godspeed little brother!' Welcome! Welcome!"

"Help me little brother! Help me little brother!"

"I will try, I will try," sang the skylark as he unfolded his wings and flew away with a trill of joy, "I will trrrrrry!"

My eyes followed the skylark as he flew away towards the line of blue hills I could just see through the Gothic archway. How well I knew those hills from the paintings of Fra Angelico! The same silver grey olive trees, the same sombre cypresses standing out against the soft evening sky. I heard the bells of Assisi ringing the Angelus and there he came, the pale Umbrian saint, slowly descending the winding hill path with brother Leo and brother Leonardo at his side. Swift-winged birds fluttered and sang round his head, others fed from his outstretched hands, others nestled fearlessly among the folds of his cassock. St. Francis stood still by my side and looked at my judges with his wonderful eyes, those eyes that neither God nor man nor beast could meet with anger in theirs.

Moses sank down in his seat letting fall his Ten Commandments.

"Always he," he murmured bitterly. "Always he, the frail dreamer with his flock of birds and his following of beggars and outcasts. So frail and yet strong enough to stay Thy avenging hand, O Lord! Art Thou then not Jehovah, the jealous God, who descended in fire and smoke on Mount Sinai and made the people of Israel tremble with awe? Was it not Thy anger that bade me stretch forth my avenging rod to smite every herb in the field and break every tree that all men and beasts should die? Was it not Thy voice that spake in my Ten Commandments? Who will fear the flash of Thy lightning, O Lord! if the thunder of Thy wrath can be silenced by the twitter of a bird?"

My head sank on St. Francis' shoulder.

I was dead, and I did not know it.

AXEL MUNTHE (1857–1949), Sweden

THE CALADRIUS

SOME PEOPLE SAY that this bird actually exists. Réau states that it is a kind of white plover which has been transformed into a fabulous bird. No plover, as far as I know, will sit on your bed when you are ill and tell you by its glance whether you are to live or die. Moreover, this bird was very class-conscious and discriminatory about its patients: you would not have been able to get a caladrius under the health insurance plan or with the Blue Cross. It only visited royalty, and for this reason in illustrations of the bird making its famous ocular diagnosis the patient often has a splendid crown on his head, however uncomfortable it might have been to wear in bed. According to most accounts, if the bird looked away from the patient, he would die; if it looked at him, he would recover; in some cases the bird effected a rapid cure by popping its beak in the sick man's mouth, transferring the disease to itself, and flying away with it to the sun; in other cases hypnosis seems to have been used. Sometimes the disease was specified. Jaundice used to be called "the royal disease" perhaps because the patient turned the color of gold or got the

Caladrius, Peterborough Bestiary MS53 (early 14th century)

disease as a result of rich living, or because the sufferer was the more easily cured by good wine and the food of kings, as Isidore said. Naturally, this disease merited the attention of the caladrius. The bird was also believed to cure blindness either with its dung or with the marrow in its thigh bone.

In antiquity, as T.H. White observes, the bird was assumed "to be everything from a white parrot to a wood-pecker or a seagull, but there was a general agreement that it was a bird of the rivers." White himself thought that the cal-adrius was a white wagtail. Identification must have been made more difficult by the fact that, as Suidas explained at the end of the tenth century, "Bird sellers were reluctant to dis-play a caladrius except for immediate cash, lest the bird's glance might heal the intended purchaser free of charge."

The emphasis on the Verses in the Psalms in which God either turns His face away or is exhorted to turn His face toward man support the symbolism. In consequence, as Hippeau observes, the caladrius was frequently employed as a symbol of justice or of divine clemency. In a fourteenth-cen-tury *Bestiaire d'Amour* by Richard de Fournival the love-sick writer thinks of his lady as the caladrius. If she turns away from him he will die. The lady replies that she wishes she were the bird because then she could avoid getting pregnant: "If I were as wise as the caladrius which you tell me about, I should not have to beware of bringing forth that which is so pleasant to conceive. Ha! True God! Guard me from conceiv-ing anything which would be dangerous to bring forth!"

BERYL ROWLAND (1918–2003), Scotland/Canada

Buffleheads, J.F. Lansdowne (1937–), Canada

Bufflehead

EVERYONE SANG

Everyone suddenly burst out singing;
And I was filled with such delight
As prisoned birds must find in freedom
Winging wildly across the white
Orchards and dark green fields; on; on; and out of sight.

Everyone's voice was suddenly lifted,
And beauty came like the setting sun.
My heart was shaken with tears, and horror
Drifted away . . . O but every one
Was a bird; and the song was wordless; the singing will never
   be done.

SIEGFRIED SASSOON (1886–1967), England

Approaching the Mecklenburg trench, Bandoviller, France, 1918

Abrahams, Roger D. (Ed.). *Afro-American Folktales: Stories from Black Traditions in the New World*. New York: Pantheon, 1985. Compilation copyright © 1985 Roger D. Abrahams. Reprinted by permission of the American Folklore Society.

Adcock, Fleur (Ed.). *The Virgin and the Nightingale: Medieval Latin Poems*. Tarset, Northumberland: Bloodaxe Books, 1983. Reprinted by permission of Bloodaxe Books Ltd.

Aeschylus. *The Oresteia*. Excerpt translated by Joe Milk. Reprinted by the kind permission of Joe Milk's estate.

Allen, Glover Morrill. *Birds and Their Attributes*. New York: Dover, 1962.

Aristotle. In *Lives of Eminent Philosophers* by Diogenes Laertius. Book 5, Section 18.

Asbjørnsen, Peter Christen and Jørgen Moe. *East o' the Sun and West o' the Moon: Fifty-Nine Norwegian Folk Tales from the Collection of Peter Christen Asbjørnsen and Jørgen Moe*. Translated by George Webbe Dasent. New York: Dover, 1970. Copyright © 1970 by Dover Publications.

Atwood, Margaret. *True Stories*. Toronto: Oxford University Press, 1981. Copyright © Margaret Atwood 1981. Reproduced by the kind permission of Margaret Atwood.

Bassani, Giorgio. *The Heron*. Translated by William Weaver. Copyright © by Giorgio Bassani 1968. Translation © by Harcourt Brace Jovanovich Inc., 1970. Reprinted by permission of A M Heath on behalf of the author.

Bates, Henry Walter. *The Naturalist on the River Amazons*. New York: The Humboldt Publishing Co. Available at: http://www.gutenberg.org/etext/2440

Bede, The Venerable. *Ecclesiastical History of the English Nation*. Book II, Chapter XIII. Available at http://www.ccel.org/b/bede/history

Bedichek, Roy. *Adventures with a Texas Naturalist*. Revised edition. Austin: University of Texas Press, 1994. New (revised) edition copyright © 1961 by Lillian G. Bedichek, renewed 1989. Reproduced by permission of the University of Texas Press.

Beebe, Charles William. *Jungle Peace*. New York: Henry Holt, 1917.

Berlin, Isaiah. *Letters 1928–1946*. Edited by Henry Hardy. Cambridge: Cambridge University Press, 2004. Copyright © The Isaiah Berlin Literary Trust 2004. Reproduced with the kind permission of Curtis Brown on behalf of The Isaiah Berlin Literary Trust.

Bible. King James Version.

Bierhorst, John (Ed.). *Latin American Folktales: Stories from Hispanic and Indian Traditions*. New York: Pantheon, 2002. Copyright © 2002 by John Bierhorst. Used by permission of Pantheon Books, a division of Random House Inc.

Blake, William. From "Auguries of Innocence." Available at: http://www.poetryloverspage.com/

Bock, Carl. *The Headhunters of Borneo*. Singapore: Oxford University Press, 1985.

Boswell, Hazel. *Legends of Quebec: From the Land of the Golden Dog*. Toronto: M&S, 1966. Copyright © 1966 by Hazel De Lotbinière Boswell.

Bruford, A. J. and D. A. MacDonald (Eds.). *Scottish Traditional Tales*. Edinburgh: Birlinn, 1994. Copyright © Donald A. MacDonald & Estate of Alan J. Bruford. Reprinted by permission of Birlinn Limited.

Buffon, Georges Louis Leclerc, Comte de. In H. D. Symonds, *Natural History Of Birds, Fish, etc.* Six volumes (1808–1816).

Caeiro, Alberto (Fernando Pessoa). *Poems of Fernando Pessoa*. Translated and edited by Edwin Honig and Susan M. Brown. San Francisco: City Lights Books, 1998. Translations copyright © 1986 by Edwin Honig and Susan M. Brown. Reprinted by permission of City Lights Books.

Calvino, Italo. *Difficult Loves*. New York: Harvest/HBJ Book, 1985. In North America, Copyright © 1949 by Giulio Einaudi editore, Torino. Copyright © 1958 by Giulio Einaudi editore s.p.a. Torino. English translation copyright © 1984 by Harcourt, Inc. Reprinted by permission of Harcourt, Inc. In ROW, Copyright © 1984 Italo Calvino. Reproduced by permission of The Wylie Agency (UK) Ltd.

Canetti, Elias. *The Agony of Flies: Notes and Notations*. Bilingual edition. Translated by H. F. Broch de Rothermann. New York: FSG, 1994. Copyright © 1992 by Elias Canetti, Zürich. English translation copyright © by Farrar, Straus and Giroux, Inc. Reprinted by permission of Farrar, Straus and Giroux, LLC., and Carl Hanser Verlag.

Carroll, Lewis. From "Jabberwocky." Available at: http://www.englishlibrary.org/poetry_carroll.html

Casanova de Siengalt, Jacques. *The Memoirs of Casanova: Vol. 5d, London to Berlin*. Available at http://www.classic-literature.co.uk

Chatwin, Bruce. *In Patagonia*. London: Picador, 1979. Copyright © Bruce Chatwin 1977. Used by permission of The Random House Group Limited and Gillon Aitken Associates.

Chatwin, Bruce. *What Am I Doing Here?* Reprinted by permission of Gillon Aitken Associates Ltd., and The Random House Group Limited.

Commonplace Book. Folger V. a. 241. Transcription by Elizabeth Harvey. Reprinted by permission of the Folger Shakespeare Library.

Cowper, William. Available at http://www.fullbooks.com/The-Home-Book-of-Verse-Volume-36.html

Darwin, Charles. Available at http://darwin.thefreelibrary.com

de Champlain, Samuel. Available at: http://library.beau.org/gutenberg/etext04/7vcv310.txt

de la Ville de Mirmont, Jean. Translated by Ian Higgins. In *The Lost Voices of World War 1: An International Anthology of Writers, Poets, and Playwrights.* Edited by Tim Cross. London: Bloomsbury, 1988. Compilation copyright © 1988 by Tim Cross. Translation copyright © Ian Higgins. Reprinted by the kind permission of Bloomsbury Publishing Plc.

Dijkstra, Bram. *Idols of Perversity: Fantasies of Feminine Evil in Fin-de-Siecle Culture.* New York: Oxford University Press, 1986. Copyright © 1986 by Bram Dijkstra. Used by permission of Oxford University Press, Inc.

Douglas, Charles Edward. *Mr Explorer Douglas.* Edited by John Pascoe. Revised by Graham Langton. Christchurch, New Zealand: Canterbury University Press, 2000. Reproduced by the kind permission of Canterbury University Press.

Eliot, T. S. *Four Quartets.* London: Faber, 1955. Copyright © 1936 by Harcourt, Inc. and renewed 1964 by T. S. Eliot. Reprinted by permission of Harcourt Inc., and Faber and Faber.

Euripides. From *Hippolytus.* In *Bartlett's Quotations.*

Fabre, J. Henri. *The Life of the Grasshopper.* Translated by Alexander Teixeira de Mattos. Toronto: McClelland, Goodchild & Stewart, 1917.

Fermor, Patrick Leigh. *The Traveller's Tree: Island-Hopping Through the Caribbean in the 1940's.* London: John Murray, 1951. Reprinted by the kind permission of Sheil Land Associates Ltd.

Ferron, Jacques. *Selected Tales of Jacques Ferron.* Translated by Betty Bednarski. Toronto: Anansi, 1984. Copyright © 1984, House of Anansi Press Limited. Reproduced by permission of House of Anansi Press Inc.

Galeano, Eduardo. *Memory of Fire:* Vol. 2, *Faces and Masks.* Translated by Cedric Belfrage. New York: Pantheon, 1987. Translation copyright © 1987 by Cedric Belfrage. Used by permission of Pantheon Books, a division of Random House, Inc.

Gibson, Graeme. *Perpetual Motion*. Toronto: Emblem/McClelland & Stewart, 2003. Copyright © 1982 by Graeme Gibson. Reproduced by the kind permission of Graeme Gibson.

Gilmore, Inez Haynes. *Angel Island*. Available at http://www.full-books.com/Angel-Island1.html

Hardy, Thomas. Available at http://www.englishverse.com

Hartley, Dorothy. *Food in England*. London: Futura/MacDonald & Co, 1985. Copyright © 1954 Dorothy Hartley. Reproduced by permission of Time Warner Books UK and Sheil Land Associates, Ltd.

Holmgren, Virginia. *Birdwalk Through the Bible*. New York: Dover, 1988. Copyright © 1972 by Virginia C. Holmgren. Reproduced by the kind permission of Karen Kaseberg.

Hughes, Ted. *Crow: From the Life and Songs of the Crow*. London: Faber, 1995. Copyright © Ted Hughes, 1970, 1972. Reprinted by permission of Faber and Faber, Ltd.

Jamie, Kathleen. *Mr and Mrs Scotland Are Dead: Poems 1980–1994*. Tarset, Northumberland: Bloodaxe Books, 2002. Copyright © Kathleen Jamie 1994. Reproduced by permission of Bloodaxe Books Ltd.

Jeffers, Robinson. *Selected Poetry of Robinson Jeffers*. New York: Random House, 1959. Copyright © 1928 and renewed 1956 by Robinson Jeffers. Used by permission of Random House, Inc.

Johnson, Samuel. Available at: http://www.gutenberg.org/dirs/etext05/8jhn210.txt

Kafka, Franz. Available at http://www.bradcolbourne.com/vulture.txt

Lewis, Norman. *Naples '44: An Intelligence Officer in the Italian Labyrinth*. London: Eland, 1983. Copyright © Norman Lewis. Reproduced by permission of the author c/o Rogers, Coleridge & White Ltd.

Lopez, Barry Holstun. *Crossing Open Ground*. New York: Vintage, 1989. Copyright © 1988 by Barry Lopez. Reprinted by the kind permission of SSL/Sterling Lord Literistic, Inc.

Malaparte, Curzio (Kurt Erich Suckert). *Kaputt*. Translated by Cesare Foligno. Marlboro, Vermont: The Marlboro Press, 1991. Reproduced by the kind permission of Micah Publications.

Mandelstam, Osip. Poem 15. *Selected Poems*. Translated by David McDuff. New York: FSG, 1975. Introduction, English texts, and notes copyright © 1973, 1975 by Rivers Press Ltd. Reproduced by the kind permission of David McDuff.

Manguel, Alberto. *Stevenson Under the Palm Trees*. Toronto: Thomas

Allen Publishers, 2003. Copyright © 2002 by Alberto Manguel. Reprinted by the kind permission of Alberto Manguel.

Márquez, Gabriel García. *Innocent Eréndira and Other Stories*. Translated by Gregory Rabassa. New York: Harper & Row, 1978. English translation copyright © 1978 by Harper & Row, Publishers, Inc. Reprinted by permission of HarperCollins Publishers Inc., and The Random House Group Limited.

Masanobu, Okumura. In *The Dawn of the Floating World, 1650–1765: Early Ukiyo-e Treasures from the Museum of Fine Arts, Boston*. Poem translated and descriptive text by Louise E. Virgin. © Copyright 2001 Royal Academy of Arts, London, and Museum of Fine Arts, Boston. Reproduced by the kind permission of the Royal Academy and the Museum of Fine Arts, Boston.

Matthiessen, Peter. *The Wind Birds*. Shelburne, Vermont: Chapters Publishing Ltd, 1994. Copyright © 1967, 1973, 1994 by Peter Matthiessen. Reprinted by the kind permission of Peter Matthiessen.

Mayor, Adrienne. *Greek Fire, Poison Arrows, and Scorpion Bombs: Biological and Chemical Warfare in the Ancient World*. New York: Overlook, 2003. Reproduced by the kind permission of Adrienne Mayor.

Maysmor, Bob. *Te Manu Tukutuku: The Maori Kite*. Wellington, New Zealand: Steele Roberts, 2001. Copyright © Bob Maysmor 2001. Reproduced by the kind permission of Steele Roberts Ltd.

McKay, Don. *Night Field*. Toronto: M&S, 1992. Copyright © 1991 Don McKay. Used by kind permission, McClelland & Stewart Ltd. *The Canadian Publishers.*

Melville, Herman. Available at http://www.americanliterature.com

Merriam, C. Hart (Ed.). *The Dawn of the World: Myths and Tales of the Miwok Indians of California*. Lincoln, Nebraska: Bison Books, University of Nebraska Press, 1993.

Merton, Thomas. *Zen and the Birds of Appetite*. New York: New Directions, 1968. Copyright © 1968 by The Abbey of Gethsemani, Inc. Reprinted by permission of New Directions Publishing Corp., Pollinger Limited, and the proprietor.

Milk, Joe. Private papers.

Millay, Edna St. Vincent. Available at http://www.americanpoets.com

Morgan, Edwin. *Collected Poems*. Manchester: Carcanet, 1990. Reprinted by permission of Carcanet Press Limited.

Mountford, Charles P. *The Dawn of Time: Australian Aboriginal Myths*.

Adelaide: Rigby Publishers, 1969. Reprinted in Dorothea Hayward Scott, *A Flight of Cranes: Stories and Poems from Around the World*. Baraboo, Wisconsin: The International Crane Foundation, 1990. Reproduced by the kind permission of the State Library of South Australia.

Mowat, Farley. *Westviking: The Ancient Norse in Greenland and North America*. Toronto: McClelland & Stewart, 1965. Reprinted by the kind permission of Farley Mowat.

Munthe, Axel. *The Story of San Michele*. London: John Murray, 1930. Reproduced by the kind permission of the descendents of Axel Munthe.

Murakami, Haruki. *The Wind-up Bird Chronicle*. Translated by Jay Rubin. New York: Vintage, 1998. Copyright © 1997 by Haruki Murakami. Reprinted by permission of International Creative Management, Inc.

Nafisi, Azar. *Reading Lolita in Tehran: A Memoir in Books*. New York: Random House, 2003. Copyright © 2003 by Azar Nafisi. Used by permission of Random House, Inc.

O'Brien, Flann. *At Swim Two Birds*. London: MacGibbon & Kee, 1960. Copyright © The Estate of the Late Brian O'Nolan. Reproduced by the kind permission of A M Heath & Company Ltd. on behalf of the Estate.

O'Hanlon, Redmond. *Into the Heart of Borneo: An Account of a Journey Made in 1983 to the Mountains of Batu Tiban with James Fenton*. London: Picador Travel Classics, 1994. Reprinted by permission of PFD on behalf of Redmond O'Hanlon.

Ovid. *The Metamorphoses of Ovid*. Translated by Mary M. Innes. London: Penguin Classics, 1955. Page 145. Copyright © Mary M. Innes, 1955. Reprinted by the kind permission of The Penguin Group (UK).

Page, P. K. *The Hidden Room: Collected Poems:* Vol.1. Erin, Ontario: The Porcupine's Quill, 1997. Reproduced by permission of The Porcupine's Quill.

Peterborough Bestiary MS 53 (fols. 189–210v). The Parker Library, College of Corpus Christi and the Blessed Virgin Mary, Cambridge. Commentary on the Facsimile Edition. Translated by Christopher de Hamel. Lucerne: Faksimile Verlag Luzern, 2003. Copyright © 2003 Faksimile Verlag Luzern.

Pliny, the Elder. *Pliny's Natural History: A Selection from Philemon Holland's Translation*. Edited by J. Newsome. Oxford: The Clarendon Press, 1964. Copyright © Oxford University Press 1964. Reproduced by permission of Oxford University Press.

Poe, Edgar Allan. From "The Raven." Available at: http://www.online-literature.com/oe/335/

Polo, Marco. *The Travels of Marco Polo.* Available at http://www.china-institut.org

Pourrat, Henri. *French Folktales.* Selected by Carl Gustaf Bjurström and translated by Royall Tyler. New York: Pantheon, 1989. Compilation copyright © 1989 by C. G. Bjurström. Translation and Introduction copyright © 1989 by Royall Tyler. Used by permission of Pantheon Books, a division of Random House, Inc.

Quammen, David. *The Song of the Dodo: Island Biogeography in an Age of Extinction.* New York: Touchstone, 1997. Copyright © 1996 by David Quammen. Reprinted by permission of Renee Wayne Golden.

Ratcliffe, Francis. *Flying Fox and Drifting Sand: The Adventures of a Biologist in Australia.* Sydney: Angus & Robertson, 1948. Reprinted by permission of Harpercollins Australia.

Reaney, James. *Poems.* Toronto: New Press, 1972. Copyright © 1972 by James Reaney. Reprinted by the kind permission of James Reaney.

Robertson, Marion. *Red Earth: Tales of the Micmacs.* Halifax: Nimbus, 1979. Copyright © by Marion Robertson, 1969. Reprinted by permission of Nimbus Publishing.

Roethke, Theodore. From "Night Crow." *Collected Poems of Theodore Roethke.* New York: Doubleday, 1966. Copyright © 1944 by Saturday Review Association, Inc. Used by permission of Faber and Faber, and Doubleday, a division of Random House Inc.

Rosenberg, Isaac. Available at http://www.versedaily.org/wehearlarks.shtml

Rowland, Beryl. *Birds with Human Souls: A Guide to Bird Symbolism.* Knoxville: University of Tennessee Press, 1978. Copyright © 1978 by The University of Tennessee Press/Knoxville. Used by permission of The University of Tennessee Press.

Ruskin, John. *John Ruskin's Works:* Vol. 13, *Two Paths, Love's Meinie, Val d'Arno, Michael Angelo and Tintoret, and The Pleasures of England.* St. Mark's Edition. Boston: Dana Estes & Company.

Safina, Carl. *Eye of the Albatross: Visions of Hope and Survival.* New York: Henry Holt, 2002. Copyright © 2002 by Carl Safina. Reprinted by permission of Henry Holt and Company, LLC, and Jean V. Naggar Literary Agency.

Saki (H. H. Munro). *The Complete Saki.* London: Penguin, 1982.

Sassoon, Siegfried. *Collected Poems, 1908–1956.* London: Faber and Faber, 1984. Copyright © 1918, 1920 by E. P . Dutton. Copyright © 1936, 1946, 1947, 1948 by Siegfried Sasoon. Used by permission of Viking

Penguin, a division of Penguin Group (USA) Inc., and George Sassoon.

Schulz, Bruno. *The Complete Fiction of Bruno Schulz*. Translated by Celina Wieniewska. New York: Walker and Company, 1989. Copyright © 1963 by Ella Podstolski-Schulz. Published by arrangement with Walker & Co.

Scientific American. June 1944 excerpted from "50 and 100 Years Ago." *Scientific American.* June 1994, Vol. 270, No. 6.

Scott, Walter. Available at http://www.englishverse.com

Short, Lester. *The Lives of Birds*. New York: Henry Holt, 1993. Copyright © 1993 by Gallagher/Howard Associates, Inc. and Museum of Natural History (New York). Reprinted by permission of Henry Holt and Company, LLC.

St-Denys Garneau, Hector. In *One Hundred Poems of Modern Quebec*. Translated by Fred Cogswell. Fredericton, New Brunswick: Fiddlehead Poetry Books, 1970.

Stewart, Douglas. In *The Faber Book of Modern Australian Verse*. Edited by Vincent Buckley. London: Faber, 1991. Copyright © Margaret Stewart, 1973. Reprinted by permission of Harpercollins Australia.

Swan, Charles and Wynnard Hooper (Eds.). *Gesta Romanorum: Or Entertaining Moral Stories*. New York: Dover, 1959.

Tedlock, Dennis. *Popul Vuh*. New York: S&S, 1996. Pages 63–66. Copyright © 1985, 1996 by Dennis Tedlock. Reprinted with the permission of Simon & Schuster Adult Publishing Group.

Thomas, R. S. *Selected Poems 1946–1968*. Newcastle upon Tyne: Bloodaxe Books, 1992. Copyright © R. S. Thomas 1946, 1952, 1953, 1955, 1958, 1961, 1963, 1966, 1968, 1973, 1986. Reproduced by permission of Bloodaxe Books.

Trevelyan, G. M. *Illustrated English Social History:* Vol. 2, The Age of Shakespeare and The Stuart Period. London: Longmans, Green and Co., 1951. Reproduced by permission of Pearson Education Limited.

van der Post, Laurens. *The Lost World of the Kalahari*. London: Penguin, 1964. Reprinted by permission of Lucia Crichton-Miller.

Wallace, Alfred Russel. *The Malay Archipelago: The Land of the Orang-utan, and the Bird of Paradise*. Singapore: Oxford, 1989.

Wesley, John. Available at http://www.segen.com/wesley/observer.html

White, Gilbert. *The Natural History of Selborne*. Edited by Richard Mabey. London: Everyman, 1993.

Wilson, Alexander. *Wilson's American Ornithology* (1840). Collection created and selected by Charles Gregg. Reprint edition. New York: Arno Press, 1970.

Wright, Judith. *Collected Poems.* Manchester: Carcanet, 1994. Reproduced by permission of Carcanet Press Limited and HarperCollins Publishers Australia.

Zagajewski, Adam. *Without End: New and Selected Poems.* Translated by Clare Cavanagh. New York: FSG, 2002. Copyright © 2002 by Adam Zagajewski. Translation copyright © 2002 by Farrar, Straus and Giroux, LLC.

JACKET: *The Parrot of Paradise*. Mark Catesby (1683–1749). *The Natural History of Carolina, Florida and the Bahama Islands*, 2 volumes (1731–1743). Courtesy of the Thomas Fisher Rare Book Library, University of Toronto.

ENDPAPERS: *Allegory of Stupidity*. Adriaen van de Venne (1589–1662). In Matthijs van Boxsel, *The Encyclopedia of Stupidity*. London: Reaktion, 2003.

i. *Sunbittern*. Etienne Demonte (1931–2004). *Aves do Brasil: Birds of Brazil*. Sao Paolo: Editoria Rios Ltds, 1984. Reproduced by permission of André Ruschi.

ii–iii. *Owls*. Theodore Jasper (19th century). In Jacob Henry Studer, *Popular Ornithology: The Birds of North America*. Tulsa, OK: Harrison House, c.1977. Courtesy of the Thomas Fisher Rare Book Library, University of Toronto.

iv–v. *Saddle-Back*. John Gerrard Keulemans (1842–1912). In Walter Lawry Buller, *A History of the Birds of New Zealand*. London: Judd & Co, 1888. Courtesy of the Alexander Turnbull Library, Wellington, New Zealand.

viii. *Kakapo or Owl Parrot*. John Gerrard Keulemans (1842–1912). In Walter Lawry Buller, *A History of the Birds of New Zealand*. London: Judd & Co, 1888. Courtesy of the Alexander Turnbull Library, Wellington, New Zealand.

x. *Great Auk*. Artist and country unknown. From the Gibson collection, Toronto.

"OH, THE BIRDS . . ."

xiv. *Superb Lyrebird*. S. J. Neele (1758–1824). In David Collins, *An Account of the English Colony in New South Wales*. London: T. Cadell, W. Davies, 1802. Courtesy of La Trobe Picture Collection, State Library of Victoria.

5. Clay vessel in the form of a bird. In Luiz Boglár and Tamás Kovács, *Arte indígena desde México hasta Perú*. Havana: Editorial Arte y Literatura, 1983.

6. *Greater Yellowlegs*. J. Fenwick Lansdowne (1937–). *Birds of the West Coast*, Volume One. Toronto: M. F. Feheley, 1976. Reproduced by permission of M. F. Feheley.

9. *Scops Owl*. Rev. Francis Orpen Morris (1810–1893). *A History of British Birds*. London: John C. Nimmo, 1891.

11. *Parrot. Peterborough Bestiary* MS 53, fols. 189–210v (early 14th century). Courtesy of The Master and Fellows of Corpus Christi College, Cambridge.

18. Stained glass wren and spider. Zouche Chapel, York Minster (15th century). Reproduced by kind permission of the Dean and Chapter of York © Dean and Chapter of York.

21. *The Raven.* Georges Louis Leclerc, Comte de Buffon (1707–1788). *Buffon's Natural History of Man, the Globe, and of Quadrupeds.* New York: Leavitt & Allen, 1853. Courtesy of the Thomas Fisher Rare Book Library, University of Toronto.

22. Wooden toucan folk art. Artist unknown (contemporary). From the Gibson collection, Toronto.

24. *Red Bird of Paradise.* T. W. Wood (1823–1903). In Alfred Russel Wallace, *The Malay Archipelago: The Land of the Orang-utan and the Bird of Paradise.* Singapore: Oxford, 1989.

28–29. Winged bird-headed divinities pollinating the sacred tree. Stone relief. Mesopotamian, Nimrud. Neo-Assyrian. The Metropolitan Museum of Art, Gift of John D. Rockefeller, Jr., 1932. (32.143.3) Photograph © 1996 The Metropolitan Museum of Art.

31. *Wedge-Tailed Eagle.* Henry Constantine Richter (1821–1902). In John Gould, *The Birds of Australia,* 7 volumes (1840–1848), and Maureen Lambourne, *Birds of the World: Over 400 of John Gould's Classic Bird Illustrations.* London: Studio Editions, 1992.

32. *Stephens Island Wren.* D. M. Reid-Henry (1919–1977). In James C. Greenway, Jr., *Extinct and Vanishing Birds of the World.* New York: Dover, 1967.

35. *Hoatzin.* Etienne Demonte (1931–2004). *Aves do Brasil: Birds of Brazil.* Sao Paolo: Editoria Rios Ltd., 1984. Reproduced by permission of André Ruschi.

IN THE BEGINNING

36. Aztec eagle warrior (detail). Ceramic. Museo del Templo Mayor, Mexico. Photograph © Michel Sabé, used with permission.

38. Owl created in Chauvet cave. Artist unknown (c.28–30,000BC). Photo by Chauvet, J–M., Brunel Deschamps, E., and Hillaire, C. (1995) © DRAC.

41. Guillemot egg. Artist unknown (possibly 19th century). From the Gibson collection, Toronto.

44. *Raven.* John James Audubon (1785–1851). *The Birds of America from the Drawings Made in the United States and Their Territories,* 7 volumes (1840–44). Courtesy of the Thomas Fisher Rare Book Library, University of Toronto.

47. *Cranes. Peterborough Bestiary* MS 53, fols. 189–210v (early 14th century). Courtesy of The Master and Fellows of Corpus Christi College, Cambridge.

51. *Small Bird.* Kananginak Pootoogook (1935–). Reproduced by permission of West Baffin Eskimo Cooperative, Cape Dorset, Nunavut. Courtesy of Inuit Art Centre, Indian and Northern Affairs Canada.

52. *Black Woodpecker.* E. Demartini (dates unknown). *Birds of Field and Forest.* London: Spring Books, n.d.

55. *Common Pootoo.* Philip Henry Gosse (1810–1888). *Illustrations of the Birds of Jamaica.* London: J. Van Voorst, 1849. Courtesy of the Thomas Fisher Rare Book Library, University of Toronto.

56. *Sombre Hummingbird.* Henry Constantine Richter (1821–1902). In John Gould, *A Monograph of the Trochilidae or Family of Hummingbirds,* 5 volumes (1849–1861). Courtesy of the Thomas Fisher Rare Book Library, University of Toronto.

59. *Whitehead's Broadbill.* John Whitehead (1860–1899). *Exploration of Mount Kina Balu, North Borneo.* London: Gurney and Jackson, 1893. Courtesy of the Thomas Fisher Rare Book Library, University of Toronto.

61. *Brolga.* Paul A. Johnsgard (1931–). In Dorothea Hayward Scott, *A Flight of Cranes.* West Sussex: Denvil, 1990. Reproduced by permission of Paul A. Johnsgard.

62. Craft bird folk art. Artist unknown. From the Gibson collection, Toronto.

64. *Sparrow.* T. M. Shortt (1911–1986). In L. L. Snyder, *Ontario Birds.* Toronto: Clarke, Irwin, 1951. Reproduced by permission of the Royal Ontario Museum.

66. Guillemot eggs. Artist unknown (possibly 19th century). From the Gibson collection, Toronto.

68. *Resplendent Quetzal.* Elizabeth Gould (1804–1841). In John Gould, *A Monograph of the Trogonidae or Family of Trogons,* First Edition, 1 volume (1835–1838), and Maureen Lambourne, *Birds of the World: Over 400 of John Gould's Classic Bird Illustrations.* London: Studio Editions, 1992.

69. *The Sovereign Plumed Serpent.* Karl Taube (1957–). In Dennis Tedlock (Ed.), *Popul Vuh.* New York: S&S, 1996. Reproduced by permission of Karl Taube.

72. Owl made from narwhal vertebra, Inuit folk art. Artist unknown (contemporary). From the Gibson collection, Toronto.

75. *Goatsucker.* Mark Catesby (1683–1749). *The Natural History of Carolina, Florida and the Bahama Islands,* 2 volumes (1731–1743). Courtesy of the Thomas Fisher Rare Book Library, University of Toronto.

76. *Winter.* Theo Van Hoytema (1863–1917). In Hans H. Hofstätter, *Art Nouveau: Prints, Illustrations and Posters.* Toronto: B. Mitchell, 1984.

80. *I Said Good Morning to the Rooster.* Charles Pachter (1942–   ). Reproduced by kind permission of Charles Pachter.

81. Day of the Dead papier mâché folk art. Artist unknown. From the Gibson collection, Toronto.

83. *Chough.* Rev. Francis Orpen Morris (1810–1893). *A History of British Birds.* London: John C. Nimmo, 1891.

85. *Vulture. Peterborough Bestiary* MS 53, fols. 189–210v (early 14th century). Courtesy of The Master and Fellows of Corpus Christi College, Cambridge.

86. *Dusky Albatross.* John James Audubon (1785–1851). *The Birds of America from the Drawings Made in the United States and Their Territories,* 7 volumes (1840–44). Courtesy of the Thomas Fisher Rare Book Library, University of Toronto.

90. *Fantastical Bird.* Sarah Webster (1976–   ). Reproduced by kind permission of Sarah Webster.

95. *Californian Turkey Vulture.* John James Audubon (1785–1851). *The Birds of America from the Drawings Made in the United States and Their Territories,* 7 volumes (1840–44). Courtesy of the Thomas Fisher Rare Book Library, University of Toronto.

96. *Blue Tit.* Karel Svolinsky (1896–1986). *Ptáci.* Prague: Vesmír, Nakladatelská a Vydavatelská, 1943. Reproduced by permission of Daniel Markvart.

100–101. *Magpie.* Karel Svolinsky (1896–1986). *Ptáci.* Prague: Vesmír, Nakladatelská a Vydavatelská, 1943. Reproduced by permission of Daniel Markvart.

102. *Serin.* Rev. Francis Orpen Morris (1810–1893). *A History of British Birds.* London: John C. Nimmo, 1891.

104. *Leach's Petrel.* John James Audubon (1785–1851). *The Birds of America from the Drawings Made in the United States and Their Territories,* 7 volumes (1840–44). Courtesy of the Thomas Fisher Rare Book Library, University of Toronto.

ODIN'S RAVENS

111. *Kakura* (Garuda). Kofuku–ji Temple, Nara, Japan (734). Photograph by Kozo Ogawa. Reproduced by permission of Askaen Photo Gallery of Buddhist Images.

115. *Frigate Bird*. John White (c.1545–1593). In Paul Hulton, *America 1585: The Complete Drawings of John White*. Chapel Hill: University of North Carolina Press: 1984. Courtesy of the British Museum.

119. *A Prayer to God*. Louis Welden Hawkins (1849–1910). In Jean-David Jumeau-Lafond, *Los Pintores del alma: El Simbolismo idealista en Francia*. Madrid: Fundación Cultural MAPFRE VIDA, 2000. Courtesy of Galerie Elstir, Paris.

122. *Cockfighting*. Anglesey Hunt Mss. f. 42. Courtesy of the Archives Department, University of Wales, Bangor.

129. *Heron*. Rev. Francis Orpen Morris (1810–1893). *A History of British Birds*. London: John C. Nimmo, 1891.

130. *Peacock Dance*. Albert Weisberger (1878–1915). In Hans H. Hofstätter, *Art Nouveau: Prints, Illustrations and Posters*. Toronto: B. Mitchell, 1984.

134. *The Arctic Raven*. Kananginak Pootoogook (1935–). Reproduced by permission of West Baffin Eskimo Cooperative, Cape Dorset, Nunavut. Courtesy of Inuit Art Centre, Indian and Northern Affairs Canada.

136. *Iceland or Gyr Falcon*. John James Audubon (1785–1851). *The Birds of America from the Drawings Made in the United States and Their Territories*, 7 volumes (1840–44). Courtesy of the Thomas Fisher Rare Book Library, University of Toronto.

141. *Bird Preparing to Fly*. Ohotuq Mikkigak (1936–). Reproduced by permission of the West Baffin Eskimo Cooperative, Cape Dorset, Nunavut.

143, 145. Aboriginal rock art figures classed as emus. Artist unknown (c. 2,000BC). In Robert Layton, *Australian Rock Art: A New Synthesis*. Cambridge: Cambridge University Press, 1992.

A BIRD IN THE HOUSE

150. *Barn Owl*. Henry Constantine Richter (1821–1902). In John Gould, *The Birds of Europe*, 5 volumes (1832–1937). Courtesy of the Thomas Fisher Rare Book Library, University of Toronto.

157–158. Illustration from *Le Pélerin*, no. 2329. Eugène Damblans (b. 1865). *Le Pelerin*, Paris. November 13, 1921.

160. *Owl with a Human Face*. Samiak Ashoona (1928–1970). In Jean Blodgett, *Strange Scenes: Early Cape Dorset Drawings*. Kleinburg, Ontario: McMichael, 1993. Collection of the West Baffin Eskimo Co–operative Ltd., on loan to the McMichael Canadian Art Collection. Reproduced with the permission of the West Baffin Eskimo Co–operative, Cape Dorset, Nunavut.

166. *Birdman Kite.* Artist unknown (1843). In Bob Maysmor, *Te Manu Tukutuku: The Maori Kite.* Wellington, New Zealand: Steele Roberts, 2001. Photo © The Trustees of the British Museum. Courtesy of Museum of Mankind, British Museum.

167. *Birdman Kite.* Artist unknown (19th century). In Bob Maysmor, *Te Manu Tukutuku: The Maori Kite.* Wellington, New Zealand: Steele Roberts, 2001. Photo by Mark Adams. Courtesy of the Auckland Museum.

169. *Buntings.* Alexander Francis Lydon (1836–1917). In H. G. and H. B. Adams, *The Smaller British Birds.* London: George Bell, 1874. Courtesy of Massey College Library, University of Toronto.

170. *Great Horned Owl.* T. M. Shortt (1911–1986). In L. L. Snyder, *Ontario Birds.* Toronto: Clarke, Irwin, 1951. Reproduced by permission of the Royal Ontario Museum.

172. *Golden-Collared Macaw.* M. O. Des Murs (b. 1804). In Francis de Castelnau, *Animaux Nouveaux ou Rares.* Paris: P. Bertrand, 1855. Courtesy of the Royal Ontario Museum.

176. *European Robin.* Karel Svolinsky (1896–1986). *Ptáci.* Prague: Vesmír, Nakladatelská a Vydavatelská, 1943. Reproduced by permission of Daniel Markvart.

REMEMBERING IS NOT SEEING

184. *The Swan Poet Dances with His Maidens.* Codex Manesse, Cod. Pal. Germ. 848, fol. 146r. (1315). In Beryl Rowland, *Birds with Human Souls: A Guide to Bird Symbolism.* Knoxville: The University of Tennessee Press, 1978. Courtesy of Universitätsbibliothek Heidelberg.

189. *Yellow-Breasted Chat.* Mark Catesby (1683–1749). *The Natural History of Carolina, Florida and the Bahama Islands,* 2 volumes (1731–1743). Courtesy of the Thomas Fisher Rare Book Library, University of Toronto.

190. *Black-Eyebrowed Albatros.* Henry Constantine Richter (1821–1902). Image © Academy of Natural Sciences of Philadelphia / CORBIS.

194. Bird on tapa cloth folk art. Artist unknown, New Zealand. From the Gibson collection, Toronto.

196. *Woodstork.* Theodore Jasper (19th century). In Jacob Henry Studer, *Popular Ornithology: The Birds of North America.* Tulsa, OK: Harrison House, c.1977. Courtesy of the Thomas Fisher Rare Book Library, University of Toronto.

203. *Horned Screamer.* Georges Louis Leclerc, Compte de Buffon (1707–1788). *Buffon's Natural History of Man, the Globe, and of Quadrupeds.* New York: Leavitt & Allen, 1853. Courtesy of the Thomas Fisher Rare Book Library, University of Toronto.

205. *Egyptian Vultures.* Rev. Francis Orpen Morris (1810–1893). *A History of British Birds.* London: John C. Nimmo, 1891.

206. *Sparrow.* Artist unknown. From the Gibson collection, Toronto.

209. *Linguist Staff Finial* (detail). In *Africa: The Art of a Continent.* New York: Guggenheim Museum, 1996. Photo by Jerry Thompson. Reproduced by permission of the Benesan Collection, Yale University Art Gallery.

210. *Blue Throat.* Karel Svolinsky (1896–1986). *Ptáci.* Prague: Vesmír, Nakladatelská a Vydavatelská, 1943. Reproduced by permission of Daniel Markvart.

212. *Water Rail.* Karel Svolinsky (1896–1986). *Ptáci.* Prague: Vesmír, Nakladatelská a Vydavatelská, 1943. Reproduced by permission of Daniel Markvart.

215. *Goldfinch.* Karel Svolinsky (1896–1986). *Ptáci.* Prague: Vesmír, Nakladatelská a Vydavatelská, 1943. Reproduced by permission of Daniel Markvart.

217. *Courtesan Walking.* Okumura Masanobu (1686–1764). Photograph © 2004 Museum of Fine Arts, Boston. Courtesy of the William Sturgis Bigelow Collection, Museum of Fine Arts, Boston.

218. An Athenian lady and her pet. In Robert D. Lamberton and Susan I. Rotroff, *Birds of the Athenian Agora.* Princeton: American School of Classical Studies at Athens, 1985. Courtesy of American School of Classical Studies at Athens: Agora Excavations.

220. An owl, a heron, and a crane. Louis Nicolas (1634–after 1678). *Codex Canadiensis.* Courtesy of the Gilcrease Museum, Tulsa.

223. *Sandhill Crane.* In *Reports of Explorations and Surveys, to Ascertain the Most Practicable and Economic Route for a Railroad from the Mississippi River to the Pacific Ocean.* Washington: GPO, 1857. Courtesy of the Thomas Fisher Rare Book Library, University of Toronto.

A BIRD IN THE HAND

224. *Cook-Shop Proprietor's Costume.* Nicolas de Larmessin (1640–1725). *Les costumes grotesques et les métiers* (1695). In Maguelonne Toussaint-Samat, *History of Food.* Oxford: Blackwell, 1993.

228. North Island Brown Kiwi in nest burrow with egg. Rod Morris and Hal Smith, *Wild South: Saving New Zealand's Endangered Birds*. Auckland: Random House, 1995. Photo © Rod Morris. Reproduced by permission of Rod Morris.

229. *Wryneck*. Karel Svolinsky (1896–1986). *Ptáci*. Prague: Vesmír, Nakladatelská a Vydavatelská, 1943. Reproduced by permission of Daniel Markvart.

233. *Greater Coucal*. Sydney Parkinson (c.1745–1771). Courtesy of the National Library of Australia.

241. *Fiery Topaz*. Henry Constantine Richter (1821–1902). In John Gould, *A Monograph of the Trochilidae or Family of Hummingbirds*. Five volumes (1849–1861). Courtesy of the Thomas Fisher Rare Book Library, University of Toronto.

242. *Passenger Pigeons*. Artist unknown. From the Gibson collection, Toronto.

247. *Mamo*. John Gerrard Keulemans (1842–1912). Courtesy of the Royal Ontario Museum.

248. *Laysan Albatross*. John Gerrard Keulemans (1842–1912). Courtesy of the Royal Ontario Museum.

255. *Brandt's Cormorant*. John Cassin (1813–1869). In *Reports of Explorations and Surveys, to Ascertain the Most Practicable and Economic Route for a Railroad from the Mississippi River to the Pacific Ocean*. Washington: GPO, 1857. Courtesy of the Thomas Fisher Rare Book Library, University of Toronto.

258. Folk art rooster. Artist unknown (contemporary). From the Gibson collection, Toronto.

260. *Parrot of Paradise*. Mark Catesby (1683–1749). *The Natural History of Carolina, Florida, and Bahama Islands*. London: Benjamin White, 1771. Courtesy of the Thomas Fisher Rare Book Library, University of Toronto.

THEN THE BIRDS ATTACKED

264. *Chestnut-Bellied Cuckoo*. Phillip Henry Gosse (1810–1888). *Illustrations of the Birds of Jamaica*. London: J. Van Voorst, 1849. Courtesy of the Thomas Fisher Rare Book Library, University of Toronto.

269. *Golden Eagle*. Joseph Matthew Wolf (1820–1899) and Henry Constantine Richter (1821–1902). In John Gould, *The Birds of Great Britain*. Five volumes (1862–1873). Courtesy of the Thomas Fisher Rare Book Library, University of Toronto.

271. *Curlew.* Rev. Francis Orpen Morris (1810–1893). *A History of British Birds.* London: John C. Nimmo, 1891.

274–275. *Long-Billed Curlew.* John James Audubon (1785–1851). *The Birds of America from the Drawings Made in the United States and Their Territories,* 7 volumes (1840–44). Courtesy of the Thomas Fisher Rare Book Library, University of Toronto.

280. Celtic helmet. Artist unknown (3rd century BC). In Barry Cunliffe, *The Celtic World.* Maidenhead: McGraw Hill, 1979. Reproduced by permission of Muzeul National de Istorie a României din Bucuresti.

282. *Osprey.* Joseph Matthew Wolf (1820–1899) and Henry Constantine Richter (1821–1902). In John Gould, *The Birds of Great Britain.* Five volumes (1862–1873). Courtesy of the Thomas Fisher Rare Book Library, University of Toronto.

286. *Albatros.* Friedrich Specht (1839–1909). From the Gibson collection, Toronto.

293. *Griffon Vulture.* Rev. Francis Orpen Morris (1810–1893). *A History of British Birds.* London: John C. Nimmo, 1891.

294. *Asaf-al–Daula (Nawab of Oudh).* Artist unknown (c.1830–1835). Courtesy of the British Library.

297. *Le Désespoir de la chimère.* Alexandre Séon (1855–1917). In Jean-David Jumeau-Lafond, *Los Pintores del alma: El Simbolismo idealista en Francia.* Madrid: Fundación Cultural MAPFRE VIDA, 2000. Courtesy of Galerie Elstir, Paris.

SOME BLESSED HOPE

303. *Brown Pelican.* Charles Collins (c.1680–1744). Courtesy of the Taylor White collection, Blacker-Wood Library, McGill University, Montreal, Canada.

308–309. *Californian Partridge.* John James Audubon (1785–1851). *The Birds of America from the Drawings Made in the United States and Their Territories,* 7 volumes (1840–44). Courtesy of the Thomas Fisher Rare Book Library, University of Toronto.

310. *Two Swans.* Otto Eckmann (1865–1902). In Hans H. Hofstätter, *Art Nouveau: Prints, Illustrations and Posters.* Toronto: B. Mitchell, 1984. Page 135.

313. *Rock Dove.* Rev. Francis Orpen Morris (1810–1893). *A History of British Birds.* London: John C. Nimmo, 1891. Courtesy of the Royal Ontario Museum.

316. Eagle of St. John, Northumbrian Gospel Book, MS 197b (early 8th century). Courtesy of The Master and Fellows of Corpus Christi College, Cambridge.

319. Sioux buffalo horn ceremonial spoon. (c.1850) Artist unknown. From the Frum collection, Toronto. With the kind permission of M. Frum.

320. *Hermit Thrush*. Robert Havell (1793–1878). Image © Academy of Natural Sciences of Philadelphia/CORBIS.

322. *Eagle*. Peterborough Bestiary MS 53, fols. 189–210v (early 14th century). Courtesy of The Master and Fellows of Corpus Christi College, Cambridge.

326. *Pelican*. Theodore Jasper (19th century). In Jacob Henry Studer, *Popular Ornithology: The Birds of North America*. Tulsa, OK: Harrison House, c.1977. Courtesy of the Thomas Fisher Rare Book Library, University of Toronto.

332. *Scarlet Tanager* (detail). John James Audubon (1785–1851). *The Birds of America from the Drawings Made in the United States and Their Territories*, 7 volumes (1840–44). Courtesy of the Thomas Fisher Rare Book Library, University of Toronto.

333. Pictish birdmen with head between their bills. Edward A. Armstrong (1900–1978), after Allen, 1887. *The Folklore of Birds*. Second Edition. New York: Dover, 1970.

334. *Jackdaw*. Rev. Francis Orpen Morris (1810–1893). *A History of British Birds*. London: John C. Nimmo, 1891.

338. *Head of a Brown Pelican*. John White (c.1545–1593). In Paul Hulton, *America 1585: The Complete Drawings of John White*. Chapel Hill: University of North Carolina Press: 1984. Courtesy of the British Museum.

341. *Caladrius*. Peterborough Bestiary MS 53, fols. 189–210v (early 14th century). Courtesy of The Master and Fellows of Corpus Christi College, Cambridge.

344–345. Approaching the Mecklenburg trench. March 1918, Badonviller, France. Image © Bettmann/CORBIS.

Author's Acknowledgements

To ALL THOSE who helped with this book, often by leading me to an intriguing excerpt, my warmest of thanks. Notable among them are: Margaret Atwood; Patsy Aldana; Xandra Bingley; Ramsay and Eleanor Cook; Bud Feheley; Jennifer Fonseca; Murray Frum; Dana and Veroslav Hábovi; Elizabeth Harvey; Michael Hurley; Michael Kan; Fenwick Lansdowne; Alberto Manguel and Craig Stephenson; Taeko Nakayama (Canadian Embassy, Japan); Raluca Negulescu (Canadian Embassy, Romania); Anna Porter; Silvia Reis (Canadian Embassy, Brazil); Tom Schwarz; Timothy Skye; Ali Smith; David Sullivan.

I'm particularly grateful to Christopher de Hamel and Gil Cannell in the Parker Library at Christ the King College, Cambridge, and to Richard Landon at the Thomas Fisher Rare Book Library. Thanks to Julia Matthews in the library of the Royal Ontario Museum and to Marie Korey at Massey College.

Special thanks to Adrienne Leahey for her indispensable contribution throughout. Also to Vivienne Schuster at Curtis Brown, to Scott Richardson for his striking presentation of the material, and to Susan Burns. Then my redoubtable publishers—Brad Martin and Maya Mavjee (Doubleday Canada); Nan Talese (Nan A. Talese/Doubleday); and Liz Calder (Bloomsbury).

Above all, my gratitude to Phoebe Larmore: it is no exaggeration to say that without her this book would not exist.

THERE ARE NUMEROUS international, national and local organizations that work effectively on behalf of the birds. Find one that suits you, and support it. If you belong to one already, then join another. Most areas in the country have Provincial or State and local Field Naturalists' organizations.

HABITAT PROTECTION is an increasingly critical component in any strategy to save the world's threatened birds. BirdLife International identifies, monitors and protects a global network of Important Bird Areas (IBAs) to help the conservation of the world's birds and other biodiversity.

BIRDLIFE INTERNATIONAL is a global alliance of conservation organizations working together for the world's birds and people. The following organizations are all partners in this endeavour.

GLOBAL OFFICE:
Birdlife International
Wellbrook Court, Girton Rd.
Cambridge CB3 0NA
United Kingdom
http://www.birdlife.org.uk

AUSTRALIA
Birds Australia
National Office and Library:
415 Riversdale Rd,
Hawthorn East VIC 3123
www.birdsaustralia.com.au

CANADA
Bird Studies Canada
P.O. Box 160, Port Rowan, Ontario
N0E 1M0
http://www.bsc-eoc.org/

Nature Canada
606–1 Nicholas Street,
Ottawa, Ontario, K1N 7B7
http://www.cnf.ca/

IRELAND
BirdWatch Ireland
Rockingham House, Newcastle
Co. Wicklow
www.birdwatchireland.ie/

NEW ZEALAND
Royal Forest and Bird Protection Society
172 Taranaki Street
PO Box 631 Wellington, NZ
www.forestandbird.org.nz

UNITED KINGDOM
Royal Society for the Protection of Birds
The Lodge, Sandy
Bedfordshire SG 19 2DL
http://www.rspb.org.uk

UNITED STATES
National Audubon Society
700 Broadway
New York, NY 10003
http://www.audubon.org/

Pelee Island
Bird Observatory
(PIBO)

Half of the after-tax royalties from this book will be donated to the Pelee Island Bird Observatory. If it strikes anyone's fancy to join me in supporting PIBO's migration monitoring and nesting census programmes, either by making a donation or becoming a member, we would, of course, be delighted.

Pelee Island Bird Observatory (PIBO)
Administrative Office
365 Roncesvalles Avenue   Suite 246
Toronto, Ontario Canada M6R 2M8
http://www.pibo.ca

ABOUT THE AUTHOR

Graeme Gibson, who has travelled around the world in search of birds, is the acclaimed author of *Five Legs, Perpetual Motion* and *Gentleman Death*. He is a past president of PEN Canada and the recipient of both the Harbourfront Festival Prize and the Toronto Arts Award, and is a member of the Order of Canada. He has been a council member of World Wildlife Fund Canada, and is chairman of the Pelee Island Bird Observatory. Gibson lives in Toronto with his spouse of thirty-five years, writer Margaret Atwood.

A NOTE ABOUT THE TYPE

The Bedside Book of Birds is set in Monotype Dante, a modern font family designed by Giovanni Mardersteig in the late 1940s. Based on the classic book faces of Bembo and Centaur, Dante features an italic which harmonizes extremely well with its roman partner. The digital version of Dante was issued in 1993, in three weights and including a set of titling capitals.